Language Arts Quiz Whiz 3–5

360 Quiz Questions and Answers to Review and Reinforce Literacy Concepts

Written by Linda Schwartz

Illustrated by Bev Armstrong

The Learning Works

**The
Learning
Works**

Illustrations: Bev Armstrong
Editor: Pam VanBlaricum
Text Design: Eric Larson, Studio E Books
Cover Illustration: Rick Grayson
Cover Designer: Barbara Peterson
Art Director: Tom Cochrane
Project Director: Linda Schwartz

The purchase of this book entitles the individual teacher to reproduce copies for use in the classroom. The reproduction of any part for an entire school or school system or for commercial use is strictly prohibited. No form of this work may be reproduced, transmitted, or recorded without written permission from the publisher.

Copyright © 2004 The Learning Works

CONTENTS

The question cards in *Language Arts Quiz Whiz 3–5* are grouped into 10 categories of 36 question cards each. In each section you will find 6 folios, each with 6 cards. The 10 categories can be identified by their borders, as shown below. Levels of difficulty (I–III) can be found in the copyright footer on the answer side of each card.

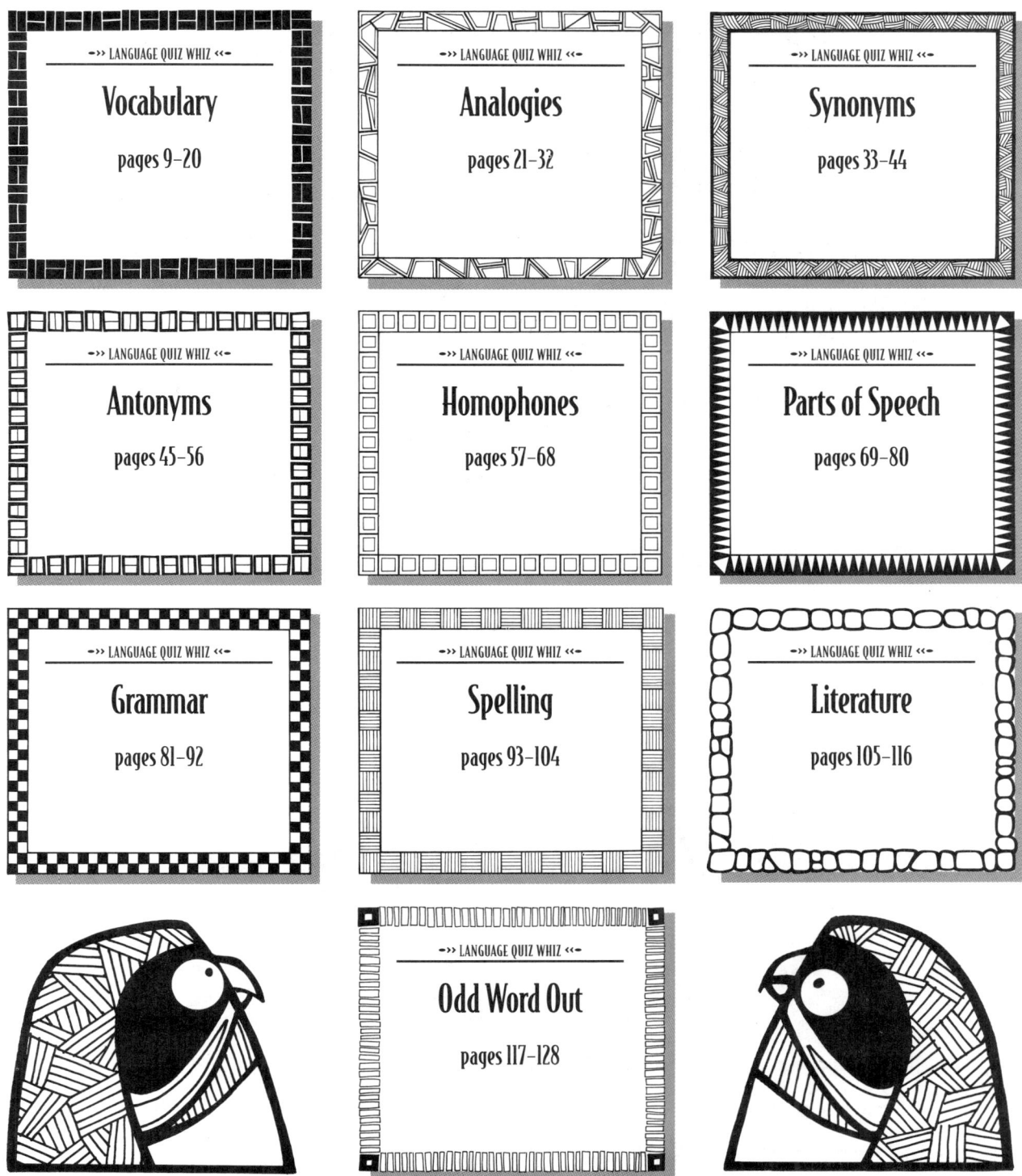

Vocabulary — pages 9–20

Analogies — pages 21–32

Synonyms — pages 33–44

Antonyms — pages 45–56

Homophones — pages 57–68

Parts of Speech — pages 69–80

Grammar — pages 81–92

Spelling — pages 93–104

Literature — pages 105–116

Odd Word Out — pages 117–128

Language Content Standards

The concepts presented in *Language Arts Quiz Whiz 3–5* are ideal for preparing your students for standardized tests. Here are some of the language content standards covered in *Language Arts Quiz Whiz 3–5*:

- distinguish initial, medial, and final sounds in words
- distinguish long- and short-vowel sounds in words
- classify grade-appropriate categories of words
- understand synonyms and antonyms
- spell frequently used, irregular, words correctly
- spell grade-level words correctly
- use sentence and word context to find the meaning of unknown words
- use knowledge of homophones to determine the meaning of words
- understand rhyming word families

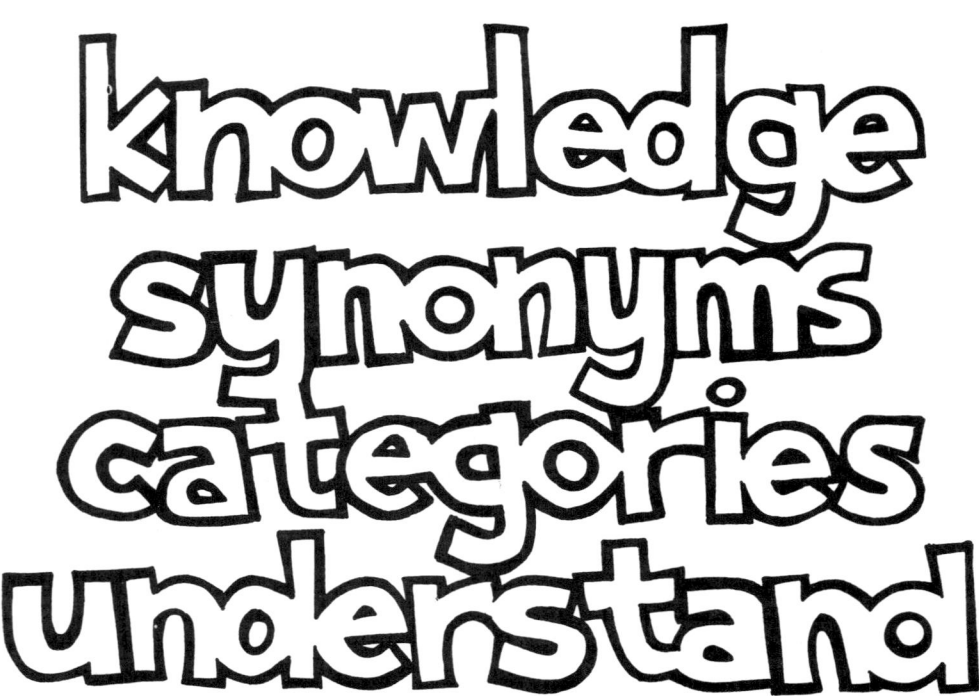

Ways to Use
Language Arts Quiz Whiz 3–5

There are numerous ways to use *Language Arts Quiz Whiz 3–5* in class. Initially, you can open the book to any page and ask a few questions to start your morning, to begin each language lesson, or to fill those last minutes before lunch, recess, or the end of the day. When you have more time, here are other creative ideas:

Language Arts Quiz Whiz Game

Start by removing the pages from the book and cutting the question cards apart. If you prefer to keep the book intact, simply photocopy the question cards from the section or sections you wish to use. For added durability, laminate the pages before you cut the cards apart. Different borders have been used to help you easily identify the ten sections.

Make a bulletin board display using the headers provided on pages 7 and 8. Select five categories at a time (or more if you prefer) and pin five question cards from each of the categories under each heading. Attach an unlined index card with a dollar value written on it over each question card. The more difficult language questions should be worth more money and should be placed further down on the quiz board. Divide each header with colored yarn.

Once the quiz board is set up, it can be used over and over by simply changing the topics and header cards and replacing question cards with new ones. Students can get together and decide on the game rules as a class. Encourage them to add their own question cards to the classroom board. A moderator can be selected and someone can be assigned to check to see if a question has been answered correctly by simply looking on the reverse side of the question card on the board.

In some sections, such as Homophones and Spelling, the player will need to actually see the card in order to answer the question. Also, many students are visual learners who need to read the question themselves rather than having it read to them.

Select a scorekeeper to keep track of money earned. You can also use play money as *Quiz Whiz* bucks to award players. Play money can be found at many school supply and toy stores.

Tic-Tac-Toe

This is a great game to place at a language center for students to play when they've completed their class assignments. Students play with a partner taking turns picking questions from the pile and answering them. If the answer is correct, the player marks an X or an O in pencil on a Tic-Tac-Toe grid. Students must play defensively, trying to block their opponents from getting three correct answers in a row while attempting to score Tic-Tac-Toe themselves.

Quiz Whiz Language Bee

Use these questions for a *Quiz Whiz* Language Bee organized similar to a spelling bee. Students are eliminated as they miss questions asked by the teacher. Have class champs challenge each other or organize a school-wide *Quiz Whiz* Language Bee.

Radio or Television Game Show

Use the *Quiz Whiz* language questions to organize and plan a classroom quiz show that follows a radio or television format. All the work of finding suitable questions has been done for you. Ask students to create an original quiz game that can be played as a weekly treat. Find class champs and have them compete against champs from other classes.

Quiz Whiz Language Question of the Day

Select one of the questions and use it as a classroom assignment each day. Students can work alone or with a partner to find the answer. Award play money to the first student or team who finds the correct answer. Play money can be found at many school supply and toy stores. The play money can be redeemed for awards at the end of the week. Another variation is to select a question each day for homework or for an extra credit challenge.

Vocabulary

Analogies

Synonyms

Antonyms

Homophones

Parts of Speech

Grammar

Spelling

Literature

Odd Word Out

Vocabulary

Analogies

Synonyms

Antonyms

Homophones

Parts of Speech

Grammar

Spelling

Literature

Odd Word Out

->» LANGUAGE QUIZ WHIZ «-
Vocabulary

What would you do with a *crate*?

    pack it
    sail it
    wear it
    pay it

->» LANGUAGE QUIZ WHIZ «-
Vocabulary

What would you do with a *lecture*?

    carry things in it
    light it
    find directions with it
    listen to it

->» LANGUAGE QUIZ WHIZ «-
Vocabulary

What would you do with a *vest*?

    read it
    plant it
    ride it
    wear it

->» LANGUAGE QUIZ WHIZ «-
Vocabulary

What would you do with a *path*?

    put it in your pocket
    walk on it
    clip it
    mold it

->» LANGUAGE QUIZ WHIZ «-
Vocabulary

What would you do with a *tuba*?

    play it
    read it
    barbecue it
    paint with it

->» LANGUAGE QUIZ WHIZ «-
Vocabulary

What would you do with a *platter*?

    sing it
    write with it
    open it
    put food on it

➤» LANGUAGE QUIZ WHIZ «➤
Vocabulary

What would you do with a *crown*?

   wear it
   mix it
   sweep it
   call it on the phone

➤» LANGUAGE QUIZ WHIZ «➤
Vocabulary

What would you do with a *shovel*?

   sing it
   dig with it
   file it
   water it

➤» LANGUAGE QUIZ WHIZ «➤
Vocabulary

What would you do with a *melody*?

   sail it
   read to it
   mop it
   sing it

➤» LANGUAGE QUIZ WHIZ «➤
Vocabulary

What would you do with a *compass*?

   put it in the oven
   find directions with it
   play it
   wrap it up

➤» LANGUAGE QUIZ WHIZ «➤
Vocabulary

What would you do with a *globe*?

   find a recipe
   find a house for sale
   erase it
   find a country on it

➤» LANGUAGE QUIZ WHIZ «➤
Vocabulary

What would you do with a *riddle*?

   fry it
   solve it
   dance it
   paint it

->> LANGUAGE QUIZ WHIZ <<-
Vocabulary

What would you do with a *griddle*?

    sit on it
    rake it
    cook on it
    play it

->> LANGUAGE QUIZ WHIZ <<-
Vocabulary

What would you do with a *mansion*?

    live in it
    sail on it
    cook it
    write on it

->> LANGUAGE QUIZ WHIZ <<-
Vocabulary

What would you do with an *accordion*?

    divide it
    cook it
    play it
    tie it

->> LANGUAGE QUIZ WHIZ <<-
Vocabulary

What would you do with a *microscope*?

    read it
    look through it
    record it
    cook in it

->> LANGUAGE QUIZ WHIZ <<-
Vocabulary

What would you do with a *marigold*?

    deposit it in the bank
    water it
    ride on it
    strum it

->> LANGUAGE QUIZ WHIZ <<-
Vocabulary

What would you do with a *waltz*?

    dance it
    paint with it
    hang it on the wall
    visit it in a zoo

LANGUAGE QUIZ WHIZ
Vocabulary

live in it

LANGUAGE QUIZ WHIZ
Vocabulary

cook on it

LANGUAGE QUIZ WHIZ
Vocabulary

look through it

LANGUAGE QUIZ WHIZ
Vocabulary

play it

LANGUAGE QUIZ WHIZ
Vocabulary

dance it

LANGUAGE QUIZ WHIZ
Vocabulary

water it

->> LANGUAGE QUIZ WHIZ <<-
Vocabulary

What would you do with a *biography*?

> measure it
> vote on it
> fly in it
> read it

->> LANGUAGE QUIZ WHIZ <<-
Vocabulary

What would you do with a *finch*?

> feed it
> wear it on your head
> fry it
> keep it in water

->> LANGUAGE QUIZ WHIZ <<-
Vocabulary

What would you do with a *tangerine*?

> play it
> eat it
> polish it
> write it

->> LANGUAGE QUIZ WHIZ <<-
Vocabulary

What would you do with an *opera*?

> sail it
> call it
> listen to it
> put it in a box

->> LANGUAGE QUIZ WHIZ <<-
Vocabulary

What would you do with a *spatula*?

> wear it on your foot
> flip pancakes with it
> bake it
> write with it

->> LANGUAGE QUIZ WHIZ <<-
Vocabulary

What would you do with a *portrait*?

> plant it
> hang it
> play it
> dance it

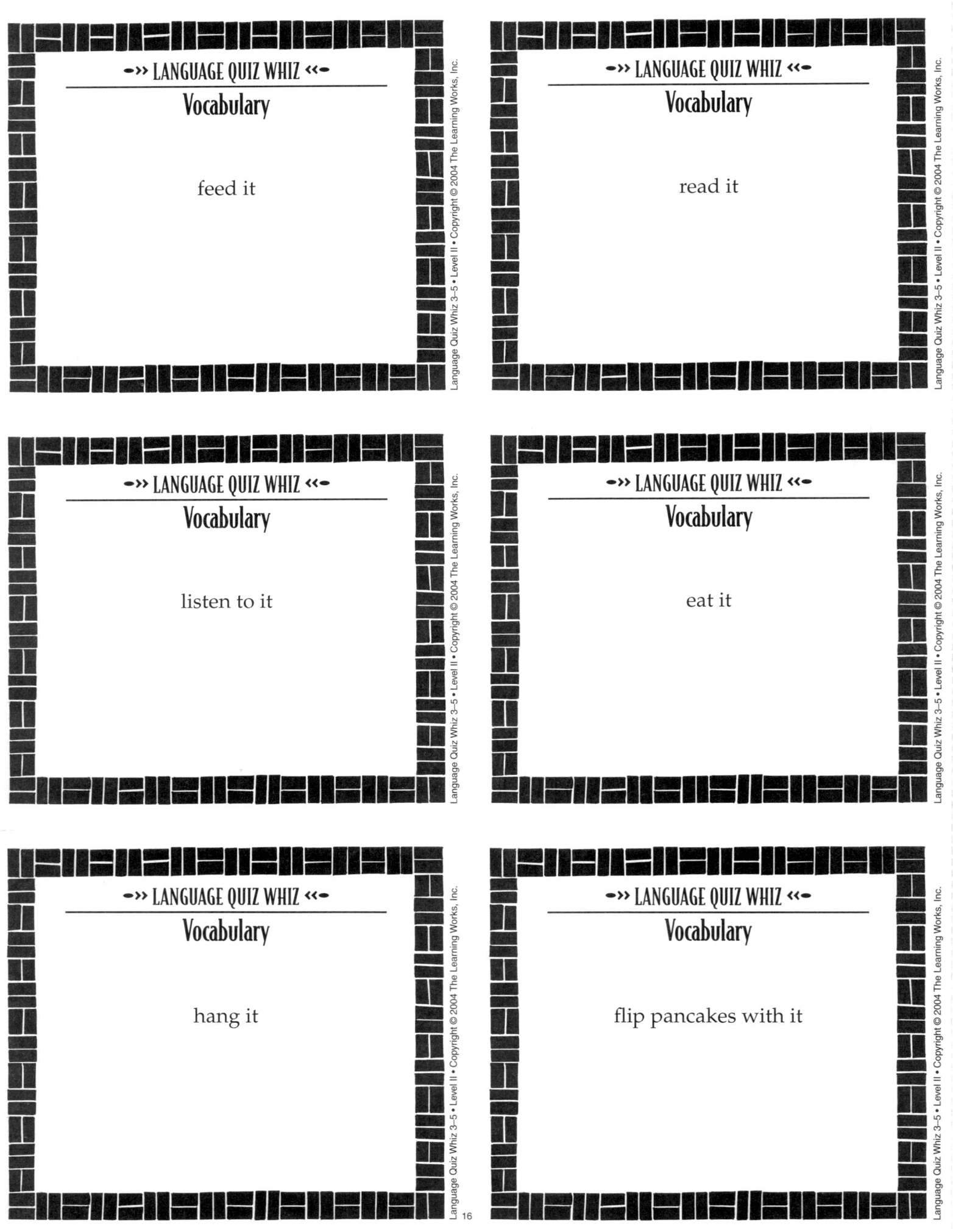

›› LANGUAGE QUIZ WHIZ ‹‹
Vocabulary

What would you do with a *dilemma*?

- solve it
- open it
- play with it
- sing it

›› LANGUAGE QUIZ WHIZ ‹‹
Vocabulary

What would you do with a *gavel*?

- cage it
- feed it
- bang it
- heat it

›› LANGUAGE QUIZ WHIZ ‹‹
Vocabulary

What would you do with a *brochure*?

- bury it
- read it
- wash it
- eat it

›› LANGUAGE QUIZ WHIZ ‹‹
Vocabulary

What would you do with a *sari*?

- paint it
- fry it
- catch it
- wear it

›› LANGUAGE QUIZ WHIZ ‹‹
Vocabulary

What would you do with an *amendment*?

- sew it
- vote on it
- box it
- repair it

›› LANGUAGE QUIZ WHIZ ‹‹
Vocabulary

What would you do with a *travelogue*?

- wear it on your foot
- watch it
- use it for cooking
- play it outdoors

LANGUAGE QUIZ WHIZ
Vocabulary

bang it

LANGUAGE QUIZ WHIZ
Vocabulary

solve it

LANGUAGE QUIZ WHIZ
Vocabulary

wear it

LANGUAGE QUIZ WHIZ
Vocabulary

read it

LANGUAGE QUIZ WHIZ
Vocabulary

watch it

LANGUAGE QUIZ WHIZ
Vocabulary

vote on it

➤➤ LANGUAGE QUIZ WHIZ ◄◄
Vocabulary

What would you do with a *kerchief*?

    wear it
    bake it
    vote it
    crack it

➤➤ LANGUAGE QUIZ WHIZ ◄◄
Vocabulary

What would you do with *viola*?

    sing it
    play it
    write it
    spray it

➤➤ LANGUAGE QUIZ WHIZ ◄◄
Vocabulary

What would you do with a *geranium*?

    deposit it in the bank
    plant it
    mend it
    open it

➤➤ LANGUAGE QUIZ WHIZ ◄◄
Vocabulary

What would you do with *detergent*?

    photograph it
    lock it up
    wash with it
    paint it

➤➤ LANGUAGE QUIZ WHIZ ◄◄
Vocabulary

What would you do with a *sonnet*?

    water it
    read it
    paste it
    plant it

➤➤ LANGUAGE QUIZ WHIZ ◄◄
Vocabulary

What would you do with a *mango*?

    strum it
    dance it
    listen to it
    eat it

LANGUAGE QUIZ WHIZ
Vocabulary

play it

LANGUAGE QUIZ WHIZ
Vocabulary

wear it

LANGUAGE QUIZ WHIZ
Vocabulary

wash with it

LANGUAGE QUIZ WHIZ
Vocabulary

plant it

LANGUAGE QUIZ WHIZ
Vocabulary

eat it

LANGUAGE QUIZ WHIZ
Vocabulary

read it

LANGUAGE QUIZ WHIZ
Analogies

early is to *late* as *right* is to

  correct
  wrong
  stubborn
  fight

LANGUAGE QUIZ WHIZ
Analogies

smart is to *wise* as *empty* is to

  full
  crowded
  vacant
  enemy

LANGUAGE QUIZ WHIZ
Analogies

quick is to *fast* as *simple* is to

  single
  difficult
  same
  easy

LANGUAGE QUIZ WHIZ
Analogies

toe is to *foot* as *finger* is to

  head
  hand
  elbow
  ankle

LANGUAGE QUIZ WHIZ
Analogies

gill is to *fish* as *lung* is to

  rung
  heart
  human
  blood

LANGUAGE QUIZ WHIZ
Analogies

canary is to *bird* as *beetle* is to

  insect
  needle
  reptile
  mammal

Analogies

musician is to *band* as *singer* is to

    song
    music
    ring
    choir

Analogies

row is to *boat* as *pedal* is to

    bicycle
    medal
    paddle
    plane

Analogies

dull is to *sharp* as *quiet* is to

    peaceful
    quit
    noisy
    still

Analogies

painter is to *brush* as *musician* is to

    doctor
    flute
    orchestra
    band

Analogies

ice is to *solid* as *water* is to

    drink
    lemonade
    ocean
    liquid

Analogies

oink is to *pig* as *meow* is to

    dog
    sound
    bark
    cat

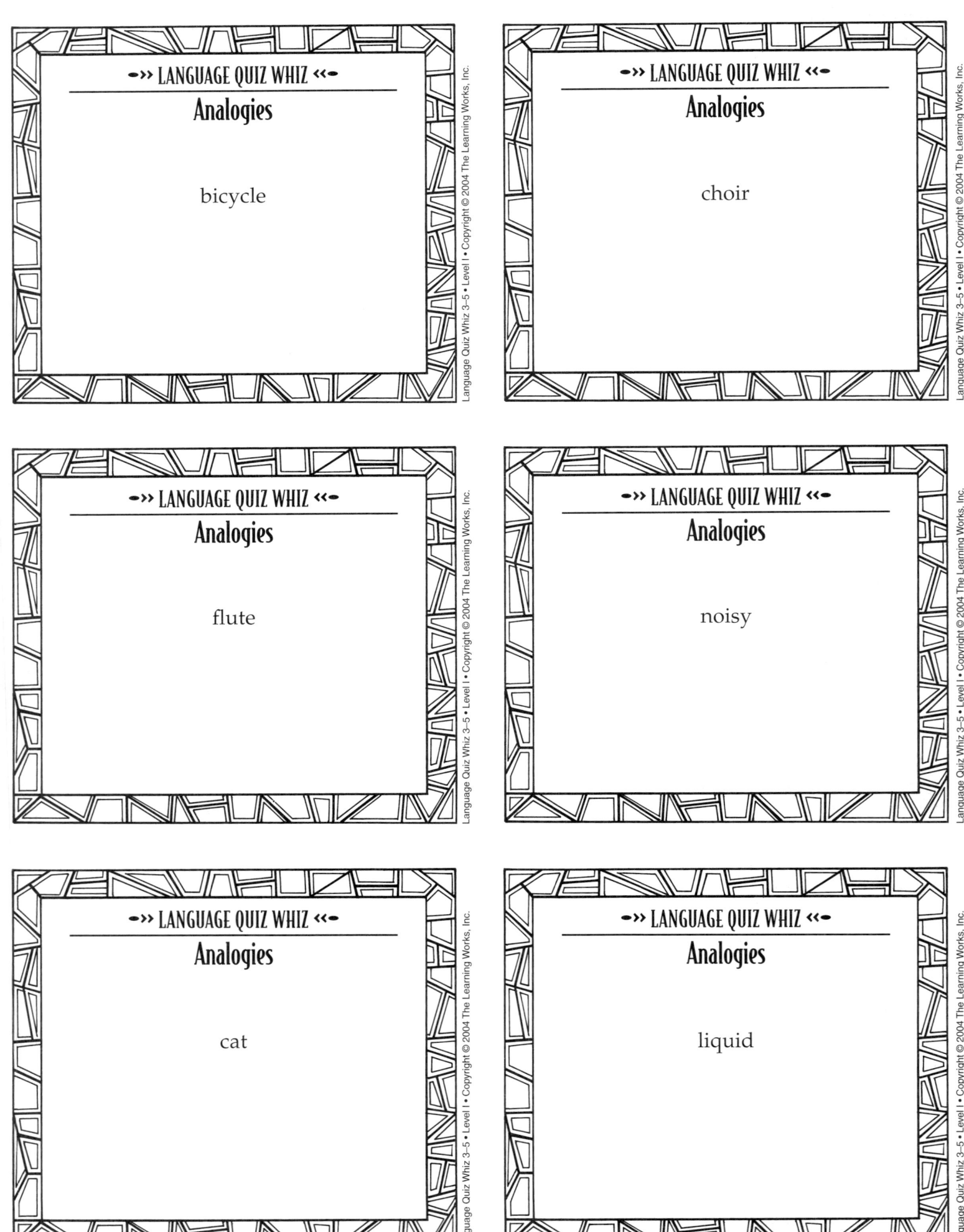

LANGUAGE QUIZ WHIZ
Analogies

listen is to *ear* as *smell* is to

- odor
- eye
- hair
- nose

LANGUAGE QUIZ WHIZ
Analogies

scissors is to *cut* as *broom* is to

- sweep
- vacuum
- kitchen
- room

LANGUAGE QUIZ WHIZ
Analogies

lamb is to *sheep* as *fawn* is to

- wolf
- deer
- horse
- animal

LANGUAGE QUIZ WHIZ
Analogies

seaweed is to *ocean* as *cactus* is to

- fish
- desert
- prickly
- plant

LANGUAGE QUIZ WHIZ
Analogies

piece is to *part* as *task* is to

- tusk
- job
- mask
- play

LANGUAGE QUIZ WHIZ
Analogies

field is to *football* as *court* is to

- baseball
- short
- soccer
- tennis

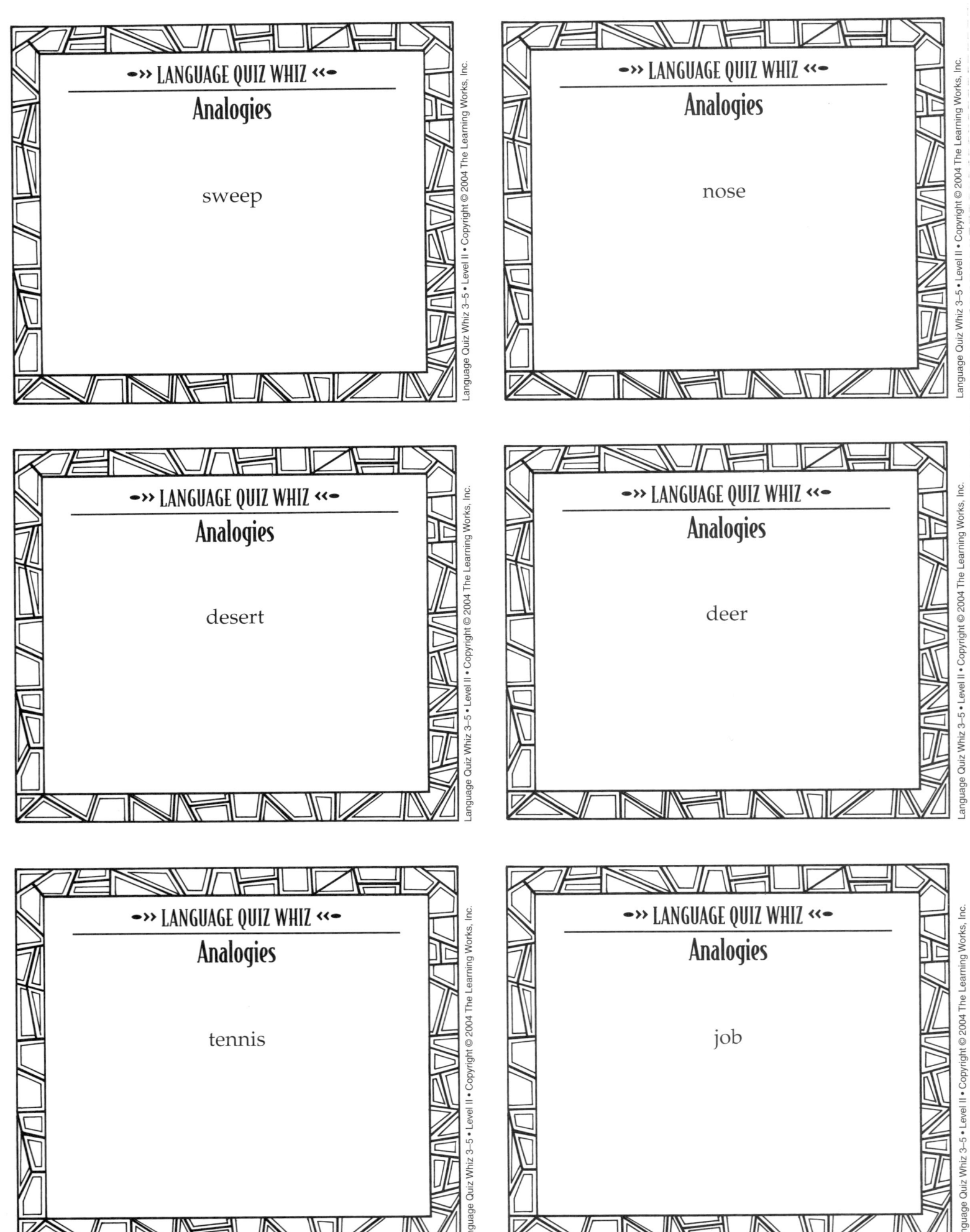

LANGUAGE QUIZ WHIZ
Analogies

student is to *pupil* as *female* is to

    male
    woman
    boy
    man

LANGUAGE QUIZ WHIZ
Analogies

camera is to *lens* as *lamp* is to

    camp
    bulb
    couch
    furniture

LANGUAGE QUIZ WHIZ
Analogies

zipper is to *skirt* as *button* is to

    round
    hole
    shirt
    snap

LANGUAGE QUIZ WHIZ
Analogies

track is to *train* as *highway* is to

    airplane
    blimp
    road
    automobile

LANGUAGE QUIZ WHIZ
Analogies

mice is to *mouse* as *geese* is to

    bird
    goose
    grouse
    niece

LANGUAGE QUIZ WHIZ
Analogies

timid is to *shy* as *wrong* is to

    strong
    correct
    right
    incorrect

LANGUAGE QUIZ WHIZ
Analogies

genuine is to *real* as *parched* is to

   painted
   dry
   perched
   wet

LANGUAGE QUIZ WHIZ
Analogies

scarlet is to *red* as *indigo* is to

   green
   yellow
   brown
   blue

LANGUAGE QUIZ WHIZ
Analogies

alter is to *modify* as *inquire* is to

   change
   tell
   ask
   reveal

LANGUAGE QUIZ WHIZ
Analogies

quart is to *gallon* as *month* is to

   second
   minute
   pint
   year

LANGUAGE QUIZ WHIZ
Analogies

victory is to *defeat* as *lenient* is to

   kind
   harsh
   simple
   temporary

LANGUAGE QUIZ WHIZ
Analogies

century is to *hundred* as *decade* is to

   thousand
   fifty
   twenty
   ten

Language Quiz Whiz
Analogies

blue

Language Quiz Whiz
Analogies

dry

Language Quiz Whiz
Analogies

year

Language Quiz Whiz
Analogies

ask

Language Quiz Whiz
Analogies

ten

Language Quiz Whiz
Analogies

harsh

LANGUAGE QUIZ WHIZ
Analogies

thermometer is to *temperature* as *barometer* is to

- speed
- time
- distance
- pressure

LANGUAGE QUIZ WHIZ
Analogies

herd is to *cattle* as *pod* is to

- eagles
- whales
- ducks
- wolves

LANGUAGE QUIZ WHIZ
Analogies

praise is to *humiliate* as *connect* is to

- join
- reject
- unite
- separate

LANGUAGE QUIZ WHIZ
Analogies

seldom is to *often* as *exact* is to

- except
- vague
- exempt
- different

LANGUAGE QUIZ WHIZ
Analogies

race is to *run* as *game* is to

- same
- sport
- checkers
- play

LANGUAGE QUIZ WHIZ
Analogies

ferocious is to *fierce* as *peculiar* is to

- intelligent
- odd
- depressed
- similar

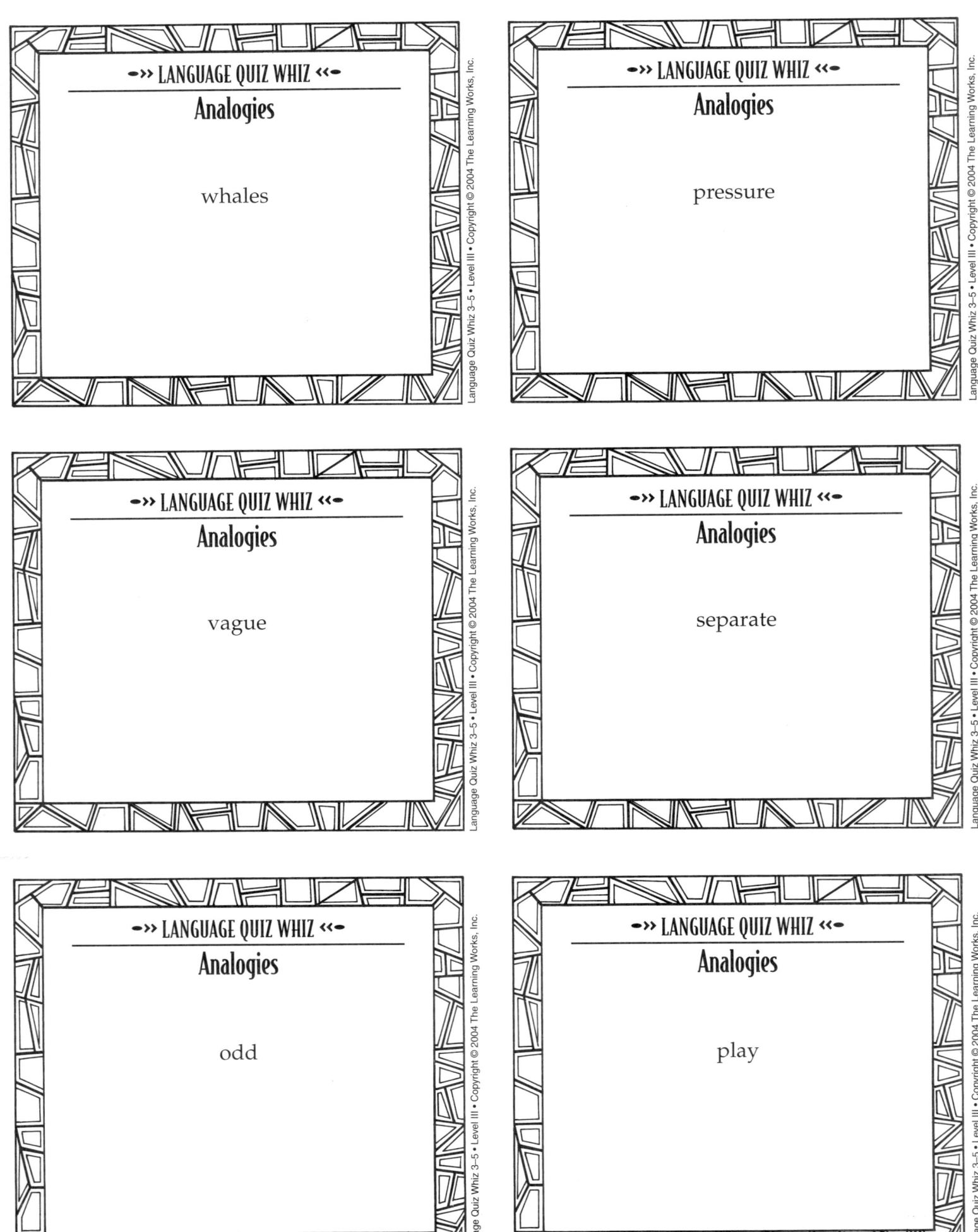

LANGUAGE QUIZ WHIZ
Synonyms

Which word means the same as *scare*?

- score
- frighten
- seek
- share

LANGUAGE QUIZ WHIZ
Synonyms

Which word means the same as *seek*?

- search
- peek
- hide
- lose

LANGUAGE QUIZ WHIZ
Synonyms

Which word means the same as *purchase*?

- sell
- buy
- plant
- decrease

LANGUAGE QUIZ WHIZ
Synonyms

Which word means the same as *begin*?

- finish
- end
- beg
- start

LANGUAGE QUIZ WHIZ
Synonyms

Which word means the same as *wealthy*?

- healthy
- rich
- poor
- fresh

LANGUAGE QUIZ WHIZ
Synonyms

Which word means the same as *below*?

- above
- believe
- beneath
- beyond

LANGUAGE QUIZ WHIZ
Synonyms

search

LANGUAGE QUIZ WHIZ
Synonyms

frighten

LANGUAGE QUIZ WHIZ
Synonyms

start

LANGUAGE QUIZ WHIZ
Synonyms

buy

LANGUAGE QUIZ WHIZ
Synonyms

beneath

LANGUAGE QUIZ WHIZ
Synonyms

rich

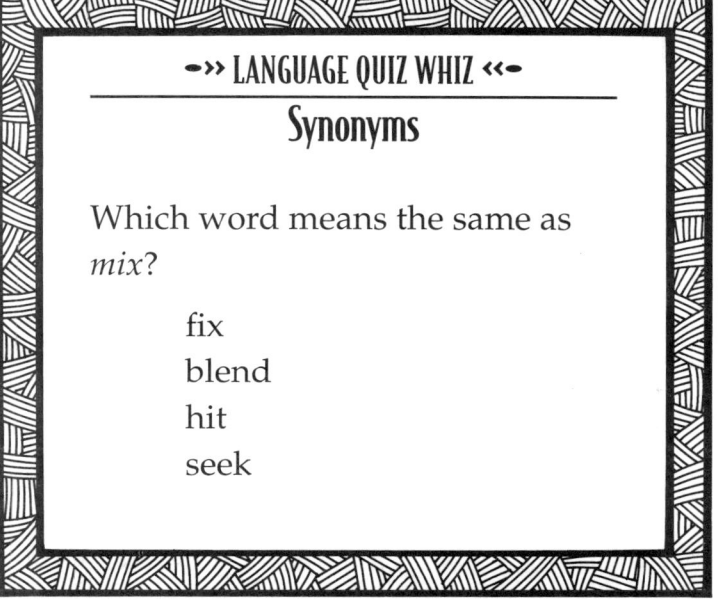

›› LANGUAGE QUIZ WHIZ ‹‹

Synonyms

Which word means the same as *mix*?

- fix
- blend
- hit
- seek

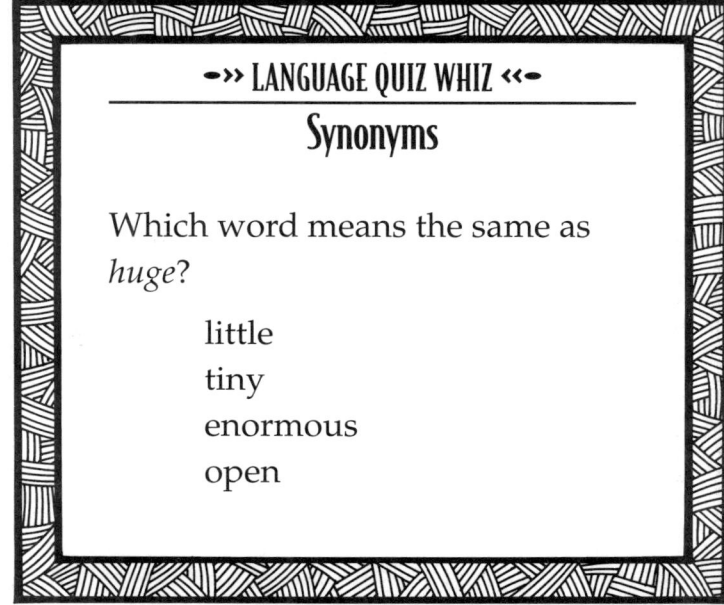

›› LANGUAGE QUIZ WHIZ ‹‹

Synonyms

Which word means the same as *huge*?

- little
- tiny
- enormous
- open

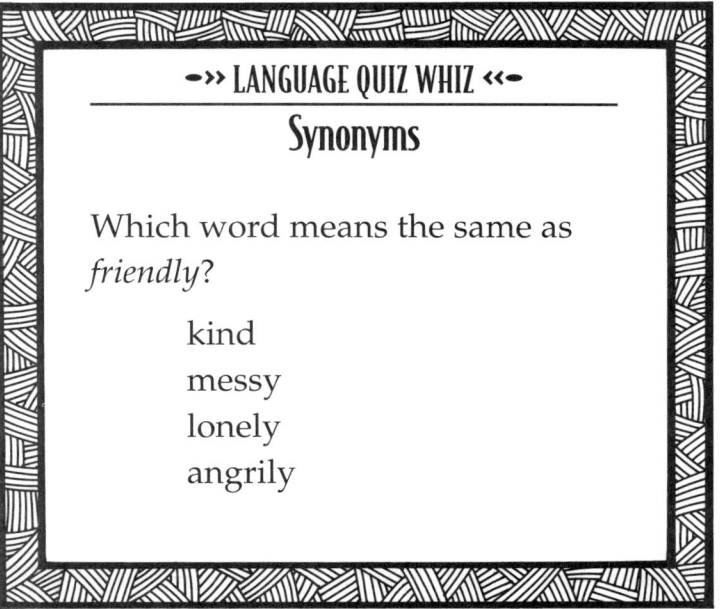

›› LANGUAGE QUIZ WHIZ ‹‹

Synonyms

Which word means the same as *friendly*?

- kind
- messy
- lonely
- angrily

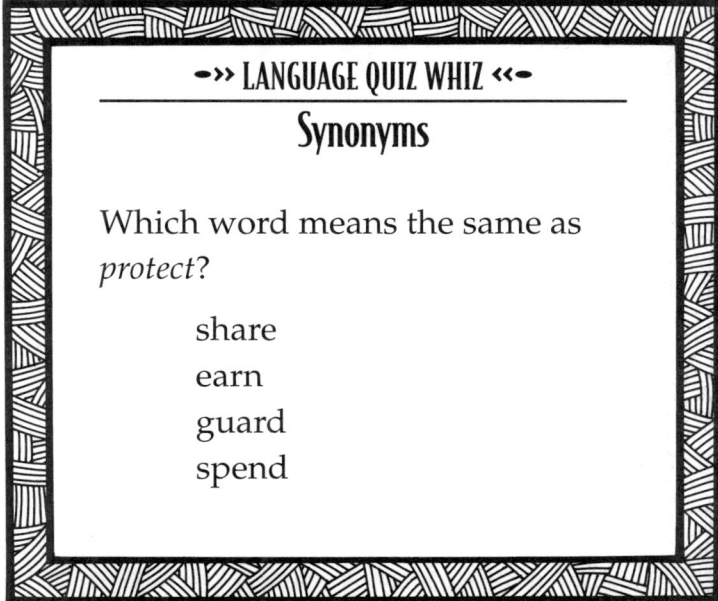

›› LANGUAGE QUIZ WHIZ ‹‹

Synonyms

Which word means the same as *protect*?

- share
- earn
- guard
- spend

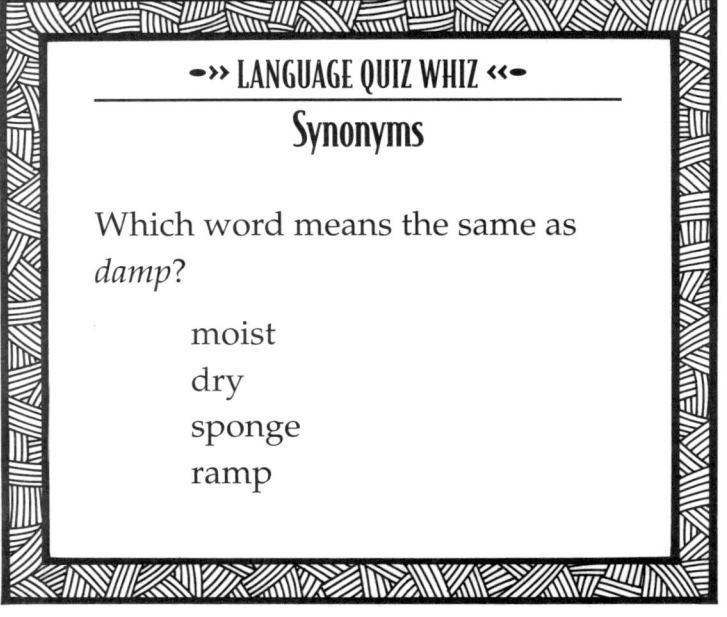

›› LANGUAGE QUIZ WHIZ ‹‹

Synonyms

Which word means the same as *damp*?

- moist
- dry
- sponge
- ramp

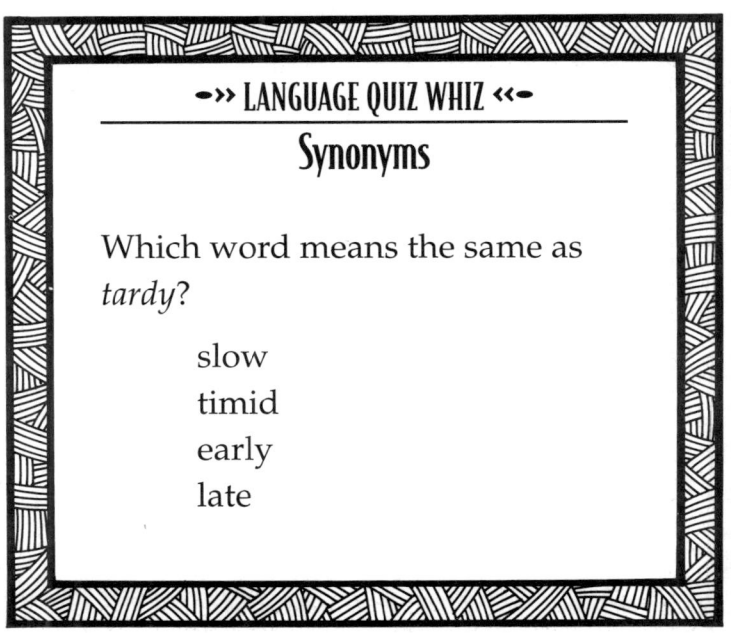

›› LANGUAGE QUIZ WHIZ ‹‹

Synonyms

Which word means the same as *tardy*?

- slow
- timid
- early
- late

→» LANGUAGE QUIZ WHIZ «←
Synonyms

enormous

→» LANGUAGE QUIZ WHIZ «←
Synonyms

blend

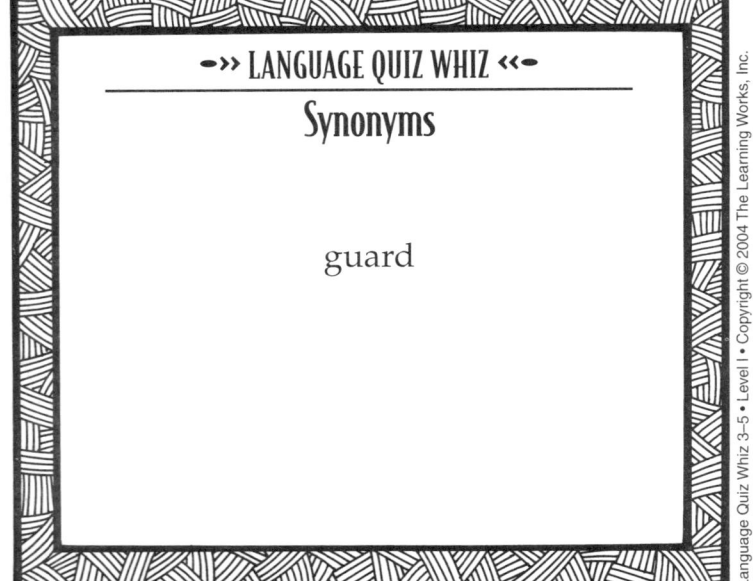

→» LANGUAGE QUIZ WHIZ «←
Synonyms

guard

→» LANGUAGE QUIZ WHIZ «←
Synonyms

kind

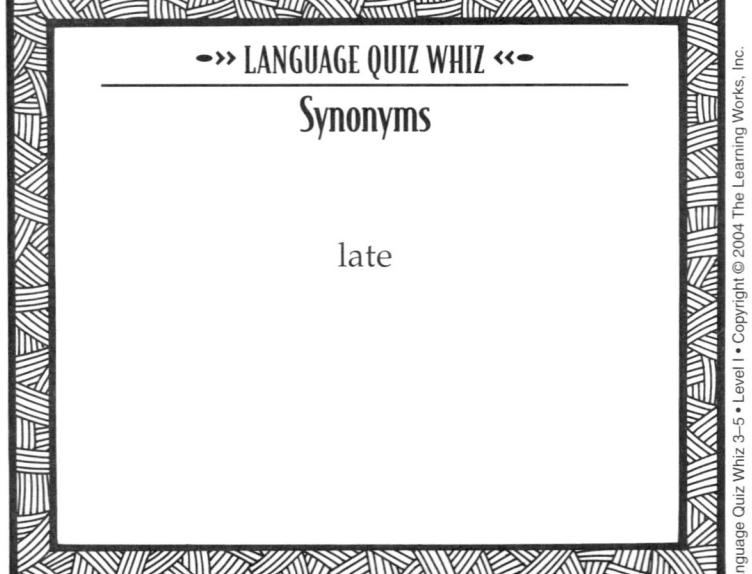

→» LANGUAGE QUIZ WHIZ «←
Synonyms

late

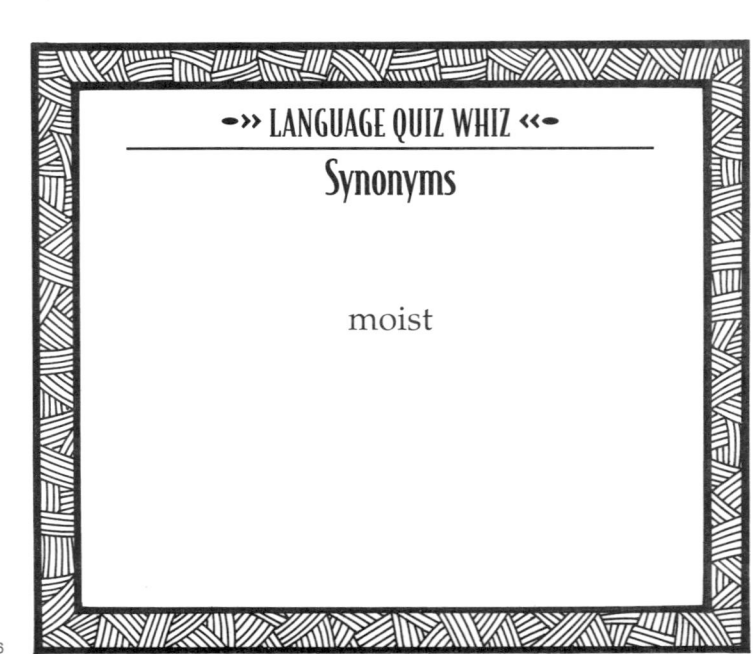

→» LANGUAGE QUIZ WHIZ «←
Synonyms

moist

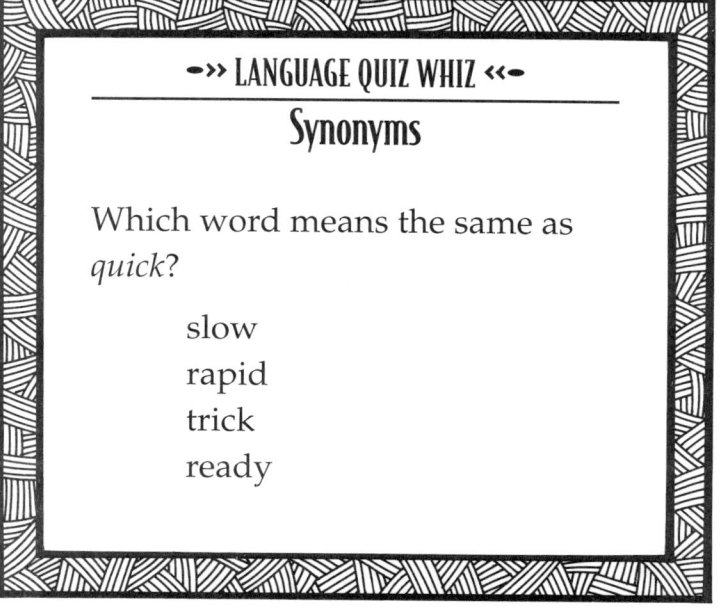

LANGUAGE QUIZ WHIZ
Synonyms

Which word means the same as *quick*?

    slow
    rapid
    trick
    ready

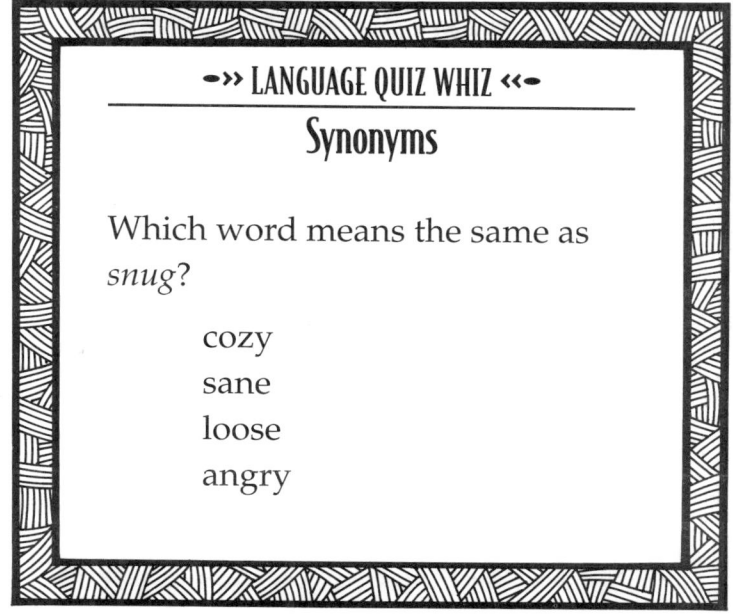

LANGUAGE QUIZ WHIZ
Synonyms

Which word means the same as *snug*?

    cozy
    sane
    loose
    angry

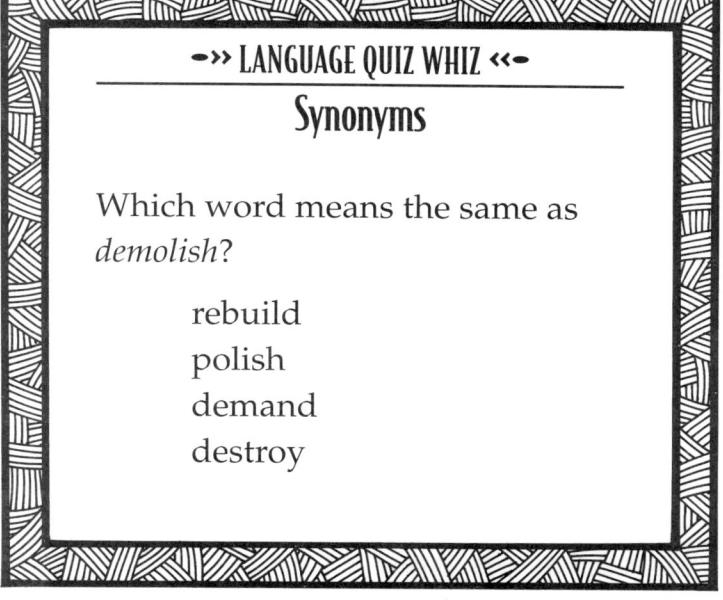

LANGUAGE QUIZ WHIZ
Synonyms

Which word means the same as *demolish*?

    rebuild
    polish
    demand
    destroy

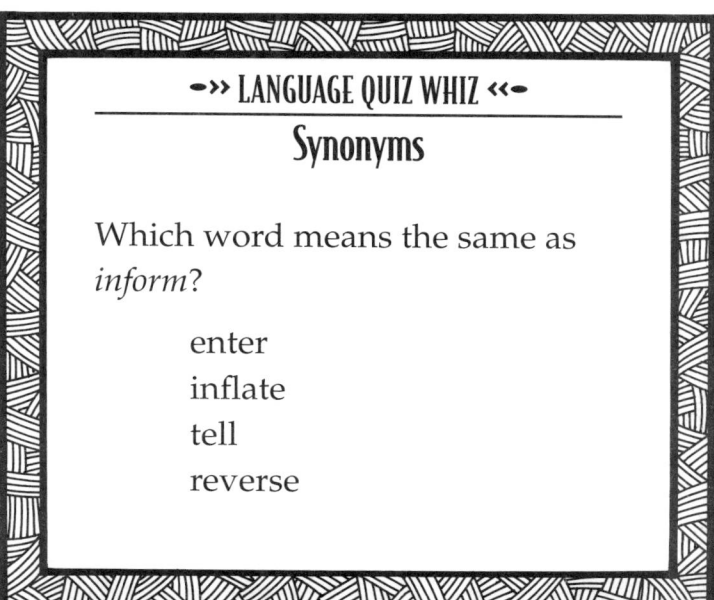

LANGUAGE QUIZ WHIZ
Synonyms

Which word means the same as *inform*?

    enter
    inflate
    tell
    reverse

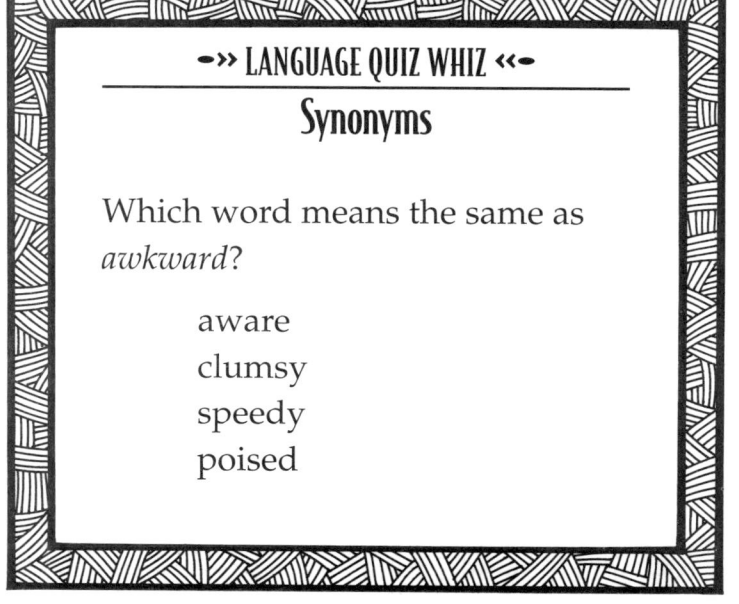

LANGUAGE QUIZ WHIZ
Synonyms

Which word means the same as *awkward*?

    aware
    clumsy
    speedy
    poised

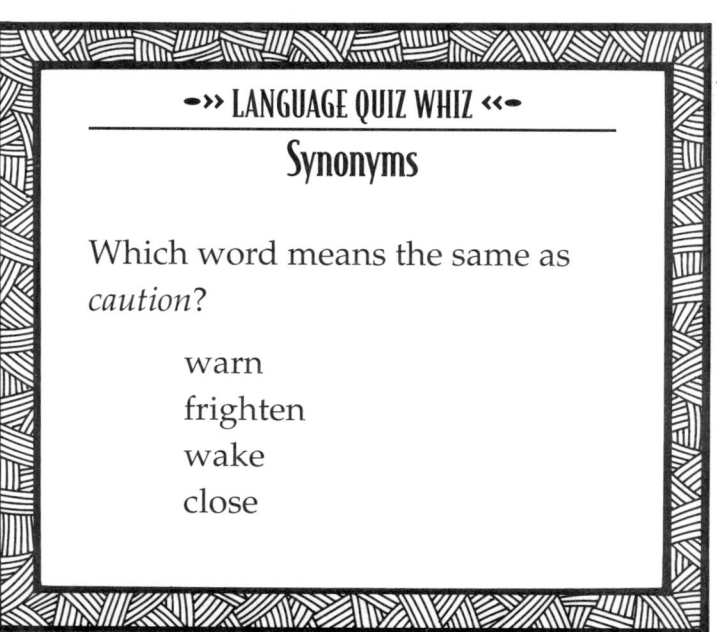

LANGUAGE QUIZ WHIZ
Synonyms

Which word means the same as *caution*?

    warn
    frighten
    wake
    close

LANGUAGE QUIZ WHIZ

Synonyms

cozy

LANGUAGE QUIZ WHIZ

Synonyms

rapid

Language Quiz Whiz 3–5 • Level II • Copyright © 2004 The Learning Works, Inc.

LANGUAGE QUIZ WHIZ

Synonyms

tell

Language Quiz Whiz 3–5 • Level II • Copyright © 2004 The Learning Works, Inc.

LANGUAGE QUIZ WHIZ

Synonyms

destroy

Language Quiz Whiz 3–5 • Level II • Copyright © 2004 The Learning Works, Inc.

LANGUAGE QUIZ WHIZ

Synonyms

warn

Language Quiz Whiz 3–5 • Level II • Copyright © 2004 The Learning Works, Inc.

LANGUAGE QUIZ WHIZ

Synonyms

clumsy

Language Quiz Whiz 3–5 • Level II • Copyright © 2004 The Learning Works, Inc.

->» LANGUAGE QUIZ WHIZ «<-
Synonyms

Which word means the same as *before*?

  after
  behind
  previously
  later

->» LANGUAGE QUIZ WHIZ «<-
Synonyms

Which word means the same as *annually*?

  daily
  weekly
  monthly
  yearly

->» LANGUAGE QUIZ WHIZ «<-
Synonyms

Which word means the same as *counterfeit*?

  additional
  fake
  real
  brave

->» LANGUAGE QUIZ WHIZ «<-
Synonyms

Which word means the same as *vanish*?

  finish
  wipe
  disappear
  show

->» LANGUAGE QUIZ WHIZ «<-
Synonyms

Which word means the same as *imitate*?

  begin
  copy
  irritate
  debate

->» LANGUAGE QUIZ WHIZ «<-
Synonyms

Which word means the same as *risk*?

  danger
  frisk
  ruin
  trial

LANGUAGE QUIZ WHIZ
Synonyms

yearly

LANGUAGE QUIZ WHIZ
Synonyms

previously

LANGUAGE QUIZ WHIZ
Synonyms

disappear

LANGUAGE QUIZ WHIZ
Synonyms

fake

LANGUAGE QUIZ WHIZ
Synonyms

danger

LANGUAGE QUIZ WHIZ
Synonyms

copy

LANGUAGE QUIZ WHIZ
Synonyms

Which word is a synonym of *hoist*?

- return
- steal
- hold
- lift

LANGUAGE QUIZ WHIZ
Synonyms

Which word is a synonym of *incline*?

- slope
- race
- gully
- stream

LANGUAGE QUIZ WHIZ
Synonyms

Which word is a synonym of *abrupt*?

- mean
- sudden
- nervous
- weak

LANGUAGE QUIZ WHIZ
Synonyms

Which word is a synonym of *idle*?

- friendly
- lazy
- sensible
- honest

LANGUAGE QUIZ WHIZ
Synonyms

Which word is a synonym of *launch*?

- aid
- start
- sulk
- forget

LANGUAGE QUIZ WHIZ
Synonyms

Which word is a synonym of *achieve*?

- acquaint
- accomplish
- accept
- acknowledge

LANGUAGE QUIZ WHIZ

Synonyms

slope

LANGUAGE QUIZ WHIZ

Synonyms

lift

Language Quiz Whiz 3–5 • Level III • Copyright © 2004 The Learning Works, Inc.

LANGUAGE QUIZ WHIZ

Synonyms

lazy

Language Quiz Whiz 3–5 • Level III • Copyright © 2004 The Learning Works, Inc.

LANGUAGE QUIZ WHIZ

Synonyms

sudden

Language Quiz Whiz 3–5 • Level III • Copyright © 2004 The Learning Works, Inc.

LANGUAGE QUIZ WHIZ

Synonyms

accomplish

Language Quiz Whiz 3–5 • Level III • Copyright © 2004 The Learning Works, Inc.

LANGUAGE QUIZ WHIZ

Synonyms

start

Language Quiz Whiz 3–5 • Level III • Copyright © 2004 The Learning Works, Inc.

LANGUAGE QUIZ WHIZ
Synonyms

Which word is a synonym of *prolong*?

- protect
- pretend
- lengthen
- prevent

LANGUAGE QUIZ WHIZ
Synonyms

Which word is a synonym of *diminish*?

- decrease
- doubt
- destroy
- return

LANGUAGE QUIZ WHIZ
Synonyms

Which word is a synonym of *investigate*?

- arrest
- invite
- assist
- explore

LANGUAGE QUIZ WHIZ
Synonyms

Which word is a synonym of *genuine*?

- modern
- cruel
- real
- fresh

LANGUAGE QUIZ WHIZ
Synonyms

Which word is a synonym of *precise*?

- peaceful
- massive
- brave
- exact

LANGUAGE QUIZ WHIZ
Synonyms

Which word is a synonym of *shrivel*?

- reverse
- shrink
- select
- shake

►» LANGUAGE QUIZ WHIZ «◄
Synonyms

decrease

►» LANGUAGE QUIZ WHIZ «◄
Synonyms

lengthen

►» LANGUAGE QUIZ WHIZ «◄
Synonyms

real

►» LANGUAGE QUIZ WHIZ «◄
Synonyms

explore

►» LANGUAGE QUIZ WHIZ «◄
Synonyms

shrink

►» LANGUAGE QUIZ WHIZ «◄
Synonyms

exact

LANGUAGE QUIZ WHIZ
Antonyms

Which word is the opposite of *depart*?

  delay
  arrive
  divide
  depend

LANGUAGE QUIZ WHIZ
Antonyms

Which word is the opposite of *common*?

  rare
  often
  popular
  same

LANGUAGE QUIZ WHIZ
Antonyms

Which word is the opposite of *strong*?

  mighty
  close
  weak
  safe

LANGUAGE QUIZ WHIZ
Antonyms

Which word is the opposite of *difficult*?

  different
  easy
  hard
  terrible

LANGUAGE QUIZ WHIZ
Antonyms

Which word is the opposite of *stale*?

  hard
  fresh
  dry
  sale

LANGUAGE QUIZ WHIZ
Antonyms

Which word is the opposite of *remember*?

  forget
  recall
  include
  repair

LANGUAGE QUIZ WHIZ
Antonyms

rare

LANGUAGE QUIZ WHIZ
Antonyms

arrive

LANGUAGE QUIZ WHIZ
Antonyms

easy

LANGUAGE QUIZ WHIZ
Antonyms

weak

LANGUAGE QUIZ WHIZ
Antonyms

forget

LANGUAGE QUIZ WHIZ
Antonyms

fresh

›› LANGUAGE QUIZ WHIZ ‹‹
Antonyms

Which word is the opposite of *noisily*?

    slowly
    rapidly
    quietly
    sadly

›› LANGUAGE QUIZ WHIZ ‹‹
Antonyms

Which word is the opposite of *cruel*?

    mean
    kind
    crazy
    duel

›› LANGUAGE QUIZ WHIZ ‹‹
Antonyms

Which word is the opposite of *allow*?

    forbid
    let
    appear
    join

›› LANGUAGE QUIZ WHIZ ‹‹
Antonyms

Which word is the opposite of *hazy*?

    worried
    lazy
    rushed
    clear

›› LANGUAGE QUIZ WHIZ ‹‹
Antonyms

Which word is the opposite of *beneath*?

    below
    under
    above
    near

›› LANGUAGE QUIZ WHIZ ‹‹
Antonyms

Which word is the opposite of *reject*?

    incorrect
    accept
    refuse
    release

›› LANGUAGE QUIZ WHIZ ‹‹
Antonyms

kind

›› LANGUAGE QUIZ WHIZ ‹‹
Antonyms

quietly

›› LANGUAGE QUIZ WHIZ ‹‹
Antonyms

clear

›› LANGUAGE QUIZ WHIZ ‹‹
Antonyms

forbid

›› LANGUAGE QUIZ WHIZ ‹‹
Antonyms

accept

›› LANGUAGE QUIZ WHIZ ‹‹
Antonyms

above

LANGUAGE QUIZ WHIZ
Antonyms

Which word is the opposite of *victory*?

    history
    goal
    win
    defeat

LANGUAGE QUIZ WHIZ
Antonyms

Which word is the opposite of *criticize*?

    taunt
    praise
    tease
    complain

LANGUAGE QUIZ WHIZ
Antonyms

Which word is the opposite of *appear*?

    inquire
    accept
    choose
    vanish

LANGUAGE QUIZ WHIZ
Antonyms

Which word is the opposite of *sturdy*?

    clumsy
    neat
    fragile
    strong

LANGUAGE QUIZ WHIZ
Antonyms

Which word is the opposite of *casual*?

    cool
    polite
    usual
    formal

LANGUAGE QUIZ WHIZ
Antonyms

Which word is the opposite of *reduce*?

    induce
    shrink
    repay
    enlarge

LANGUAGE QUIZ WHIZ
Antonyms

praise

LANGUAGE QUIZ WHIZ
Antonyms

defeat

LANGUAGE QUIZ WHIZ
Antonyms

fragile

LANGUAGE QUIZ WHIZ
Antonyms

vanish

LANGUAGE QUIZ WHIZ
Antonyms

enlarge

LANGUAGE QUIZ WHIZ
Antonyms

formal

›› LANGUAGE QUIZ WHIZ ‹‹
Antonyms

Which word is the opposite of *interior*?

- inside
- exterior
- inferior
- idea

›› LANGUAGE QUIZ WHIZ ‹‹
Antonyms

Which word is the opposite of *rapidly*?

- quickly
- noisily
- slowly
- easily

›› LANGUAGE QUIZ WHIZ ‹‹
Antonyms

Which word is the opposite of *purchase*?

- package
- buy
- protect
- sell

›› LANGUAGE QUIZ WHIZ ‹‹
Antonyms

Which word is the opposite of *enormous*?

- gigantic
- huge
- tiny
- wide

›› LANGUAGE QUIZ WHIZ ‹‹
Antonyms

Which word is the opposite of *shout*?

- scream
- pout
- yell
- whisper

›› LANGUAGE QUIZ WHIZ ‹‹
Antonyms

Which word is the opposite of *foolish*?

- stupid
- wise
- funny
- friendly

⇢» LANGUAGE QUIZ WHIZ «⇠
Antonyms

slowly

⇢» LANGUAGE QUIZ WHIZ «⇠
Antonyms

exterior

⇢» LANGUAGE QUIZ WHIZ «⇠
Antonyms

tiny

⇢» LANGUAGE QUIZ WHIZ «⇠
Antonyms

sell

⇢» LANGUAGE QUIZ WHIZ «⇠
Antonyms

wise

⇢» LANGUAGE QUIZ WHIZ «⇠
Antonyms

whisper

›› LANGUAGE QUIZ WHIZ ‹‹
Antonyms

Which word is an antonym of *flimsy*?

   forgetful
   crooked
   solid
   shaky

›› LANGUAGE QUIZ WHIZ ‹‹
Antonyms

Which word is an antonym of *temporary*?

   seldom
   permanent
   few
   timely

›› LANGUAGE QUIZ WHIZ ‹‹
Antonyms

Which word is an antonym of *moderate*?

   brave
   quiet
   strict
   extreme

›› LANGUAGE QUIZ WHIZ ‹‹
Antonyms

Which word is an antonym of *scarce*?

   plentiful
   afraid
   dull
   honest

›› LANGUAGE QUIZ WHIZ ‹‹
Antonyms

Which word is an antonym of *maximum*?

   formal
   sensible
   fragile
   minimum

›› LANGUAGE QUIZ WHIZ ‹‹
Antonyms

Which word is an antonym of *smooth*?

   calm
   straight
   rough
   flat

LANGUAGE QUIZ WHIZ
Antonyms

permanent

LANGUAGE QUIZ WHIZ
Antonyms

solid

LANGUAGE QUIZ WHIZ
Antonyms

plentiful

LANGUAGE QUIZ WHIZ
Antonyms

extreme

LANGUAGE QUIZ WHIZ
Antonyms

rough

LANGUAGE QUIZ WHIZ
Antonyms

minimum

LANGUAGE QUIZ WHIZ
Antonyms

Which word is an antonym of *advance*?

    forward
    advise
    admit
    retreat

LANGUAGE QUIZ WHIZ
Antonyms

Which word is an antonym of *meager*?

    hungry
    ample
    few
    eager

LANGUAGE QUIZ WHIZ
Antonyms

Which word is an antonym of *vague*?

    plague
    void
    view
    exact

LANGUAGE QUIZ WHIZ
Antonyms

Which word is an antonym of *hasten*?

    speed
    delay
    fasten
    rush

LANGUAGE QUIZ WHIZ
Antonyms

Which word is an antonym of *defense*?

    dense
    protection
    offense
    depend

LANGUAGE QUIZ WHIZ
Antonyms

Which word is an antonym of *ambitious*?

    brilliant
    sneaky
    lazy
    curious

LANGUAGE QUIZ WHIZ
Antonyms

ample

LANGUAGE QUIZ WHIZ
Antonyms

retreat

LANGUAGE QUIZ WHIZ
Antonyms

delay

LANGUAGE QUIZ WHIZ
Antonyms

exact

LANGUAGE QUIZ WHIZ
Antonyms

lazy

LANGUAGE QUIZ WHIZ
Antonyms

offense

->> LANGUAGE QUIZ WHIZ <<-
Homophones

Which homophone means *to find the sum of two or more numbers*?

    a. ad
    b. add

->> LANGUAGE QUIZ WHIZ <<-
Homophones

Which homophone means *a large branch of a tree*?

    a. bough
    b. bow

->> LANGUAGE QUIZ WHIZ <<-
Homophones

Which homophone is *the name of a vegetable*?

    a. beat
    b. beet

->> LANGUAGE QUIZ WHIZ <<-
Homophones

Which homophone means *to select*?

    a. chews
    b. choose

->> LANGUAGE QUIZ WHIZ <<-
Homophones

Which homophone means *a sad, low sound*?

    a. grown
    b. groan

->> LANGUAGE QUIZ WHIZ <<-
Homophones

Which homophone means *lazy*?

    a. idol
    b. idle

LANGUAGE QUIZ WHIZ
Homophones

a. bough

LANGUAGE QUIZ WHIZ
Homophones

b. add

LANGUAGE QUIZ WHIZ
Homophones

b. choose

LANGUAGE QUIZ WHIZ
Homophones

b. beet

LANGUAGE QUIZ WHIZ
Homophones

b. idle

LANGUAGE QUIZ WHIZ
Homophones

b. groan

►» LANGUAGE QUIZ WHIZ «◄
Homophones

Which homophone means *a group of connected rooms*?

    a. sweet
    b. suite

►» LANGUAGE QUIZ WHIZ «◄
Homophones

Which homophone is *the name of a spice*?

    a. time
    b. thyme

►» LANGUAGE QUIZ WHIZ «◄
Homophones

Which homophone means *a strong metal made of iron*?

    a. steel
    b. steal

►» LANGUAGE QUIZ WHIZ «◄
Homophones

Which homophone means *a course used for traveling*?

    a. root
    b. route

►» LANGUAGE QUIZ WHIZ «◄
Homophones

Which homophone means *solitary or only*?

    a. loan
    b. lone

►» LANGUAGE QUIZ WHIZ «◄
Homophones

Which homophone means *painful*?

    a. sore
    b. soar

LANGUAGE QUIZ WHIZ
Homophones

b. thyme

LANGUAGE QUIZ WHIZ
Homophones

b. suite

LANGUAGE QUIZ WHIZ
Homophones

b. route

LANGUAGE QUIZ WHIZ
Homophones

a. steel

LANGUAGE QUIZ WHIZ
Homophones

a. sore

LANGUAGE QUIZ WHIZ
Homophones

b. lone

⇒» LANGUAGE QUIZ WHIZ «⇐
Homophones

Which homophone means *the amount of heaviness of a person or thing*?

    a. weight
    b. wait

⇒» LANGUAGE QUIZ WHIZ «⇐
Homophones

Which homophone means *a hole or tear that lets something pass through by accident*?

    a. leak
    b. leek

⇒» LANGUAGE QUIZ WHIZ «⇐
Homophones

Which homophone means *to carry or have on the body*?

    a. where
    b. wear

⇒» LANGUAGE QUIZ WHIZ «⇐
Homophones

Which homophone means *to make a squeaking sound*?

    a. creek
    b. creak

⇒» LANGUAGE QUIZ WHIZ «⇐
Homophones

Which homophone means *a thin rope*?

    a. cord
    b. chord

⇒» LANGUAGE QUIZ WHIZ «⇐
Homophones

Which homophone means *a slide*?

    a. chute
    b. shoot

LANGUAGE QUIZ WHIZ
Homophones

a. leak

LANGUAGE QUIZ WHIZ
Homophones

a. weight

LANGUAGE QUIZ WHIZ
Homophones

b. creak

LANGUAGE QUIZ WHIZ
Homophones

b. wear

LANGUAGE QUIZ WHIZ
Homophones

a. chute

LANGUAGE QUIZ WHIZ
Homophones

a. cord

➤➤ LANGUAGE QUIZ WHIZ ➤➤
Homophones

Which homophone means *a hard fruit related to the squash or pumpkin*?

    a. gored
    b. gourd

➤➤ LANGUAGE QUIZ WHIZ ➤➤
Homophones

Which homophone means *unpleasantly cold*?

    a. chilly
    b. chili

➤➤ LANGUAGE QUIZ WHIZ ➤➤
Homophones

Which homophone means *to drag away*?

    a. haul
    b. hall

➤➤ LANGUAGE QUIZ WHIZ ➤➤
Homophones

Which homophone means *a wild animal in the cat family*?

    a. links
    b. lynx

➤➤ LANGUAGE QUIZ WHIZ ➤➤
Homophones

Which homophone means *a carriage on runners drawn by a horse*?

    a. sleigh
    b. slay

➤➤ LANGUAGE QUIZ WHIZ ➤➤
Homophones

Which homophone means *an animal that looks like a clam*?

    a. mussel
    b. muscle

->> LANGUAGE QUIZ WHIZ <<-
Homophones

a. chilly

->> LANGUAGE QUIZ WHIZ <<-
Homophones

b. gourd

->> LANGUAGE QUIZ WHIZ <<-
Homophones

b. lynx

->> LANGUAGE QUIZ WHIZ <<-
Homophones

a. haul

->> LANGUAGE QUIZ WHIZ <<-
Homophones

a. mussel

->> LANGUAGE QUIZ WHIZ <<-
Homophones

a. sleigh

LANGUAGE QUIZ WHIZ
Homophones

Which homophone means *the period of time a monarch rules*?

    a. reign
    b. rein

LANGUAGE QUIZ WHIZ
Homophones

Which homophone means *to carry goods from place to place and offer them for sale*?

    a. pedal
    b. peddle

LANGUAGE QUIZ WHIZ
Homophones

Which homophone means *the head of a school*?

    a. principle
    b. principal

LANGUAGE QUIZ WHIZ
Homophones

Which homophone is *another name for the belly button*?

    a. navel
    b. naval

LANGUAGE QUIZ WHIZ
Homophones

Which homophone means *advice*?

    a. council
    b. counsel

LANGUAGE QUIZ WHIZ
Homophones

Which homophone means *coming from a higher place to a lower one*?

    a. descent
    b. dissent

LANGUAGE QUIZ WHIZ
Homophones

b. peddle

LANGUAGE QUIZ WHIZ
Homophones

a. reign

LANGUAGE QUIZ WHIZ
Homophones

a. navel

LANGUAGE QUIZ WHIZ
Homophones

b. principal

LANGUAGE QUIZ WHIZ
Homophones

a. descent

LANGUAGE QUIZ WHIZ
Homophones

b. counsel

» LANGUAGE QUIZ WHIZ «
Homophones

Which homophone means *toward what is ahead*?

    a. foreword
    b. forward

» LANGUAGE QUIZ WHIZ «
Homophones

Which homophone means *a crowd or swarm*?

    a. horde
    b. hoard

» LANGUAGE QUIZ WHIZ «
Homophones

Which homophone means *a little island*?

    a. islet
    b. eyelet

» LANGUAGE QUIZ WHIZ «
Homophones

Which homophone means *an animal that looks like a large pig*?

    a. taper
    b. tapir

» LANGUAGE QUIZ WHIZ «
Homophones

Which homophone means *not able to produce anything*?

    a. baron
    b. barren

» LANGUAGE QUIZ WHIZ «
Homophones

Which homophone means *the roof of the mouth*?

    a. palate
    b. pallet

LANGUAGE QUIZ WHIZ
Homophones

a. horde

LANGUAGE QUIZ WHIZ
Homophones

b. forward

LANGUAGE QUIZ WHIZ
Homophones

b. tapir

LANGUAGE QUIZ WHIZ
Homophones

a. islet

LANGUAGE QUIZ WHIZ
Homophones

a. palate

LANGUAGE QUIZ WHIZ
Homophones

b. barren

LANGUAGE QUIZ WHIZ
Parts of Speech

Which word is not a noun?

- student
- glad
- kitten
- habit

LANGUAGE QUIZ WHIZ
Parts of Speech

Which word is not a verb?

- shady
- sew
- amuse
- recycle

LANGUAGE QUIZ WHIZ
Parts of Speech

Which word is not a pronoun?

- she
- him
- themselves
- father

LANGUAGE QUIZ WHIZ
Parts of Speech

Which word is not an adjective?

- colorful
- sadly
- serious
- trusty

LANGUAGE QUIZ WHIZ
Parts of Speech

Which word is not an adverb?

- ahead
- quickly
- carefully
- bruised

LANGUAGE QUIZ WHIZ
Parts of Speech

Which word is not an adjective?

- gentle
- gently
- generous
- ghostly

LANGUAGE QUIZ WHIZ
Parts of Speech

shady

LANGUAGE QUIZ WHIZ
Parts of Speech

glad

LANGUAGE QUIZ WHIZ
Parts of Speech

sadly

LANGUAGE QUIZ WHIZ
Parts of Speech

father

LANGUAGE QUIZ WHIZ
Parts of Speech

gently

LANGUAGE QUIZ WHIZ
Parts of Speech

bruised

» LANGUAGE QUIZ WHIZ «
Parts of Speech

What part of speech is the word *kindly* in this sentence?

Thank you *kindly* for helping me with my homework.

» LANGUAGE QUIZ WHIZ «
Parts of Speech

What part of speech is the word *hose* in this sentence?

We had to *hose* the dirt off the front steps.

» LANGUAGE QUIZ WHIZ «
Parts of Speech

What part of speech is the word *meeting* in this sentence?

The *meeting* took place at noon.

» LANGUAGE QUIZ WHIZ «
Parts of Speech

What part of speech is the word *north* in this sentence?

We headed *north* toward the beach.

» LANGUAGE QUIZ WHIZ «
Parts of Speech

What part of speech is the word *firm* in this sentence?

Mom took a *firm* stand on the issue of our allowance.

» LANGUAGE QUIZ WHIZ «
Parts of Speech

What part of speech is the word *test* in this sentence?

The coach gave us a drill to *test* our skill in shooting baskets.

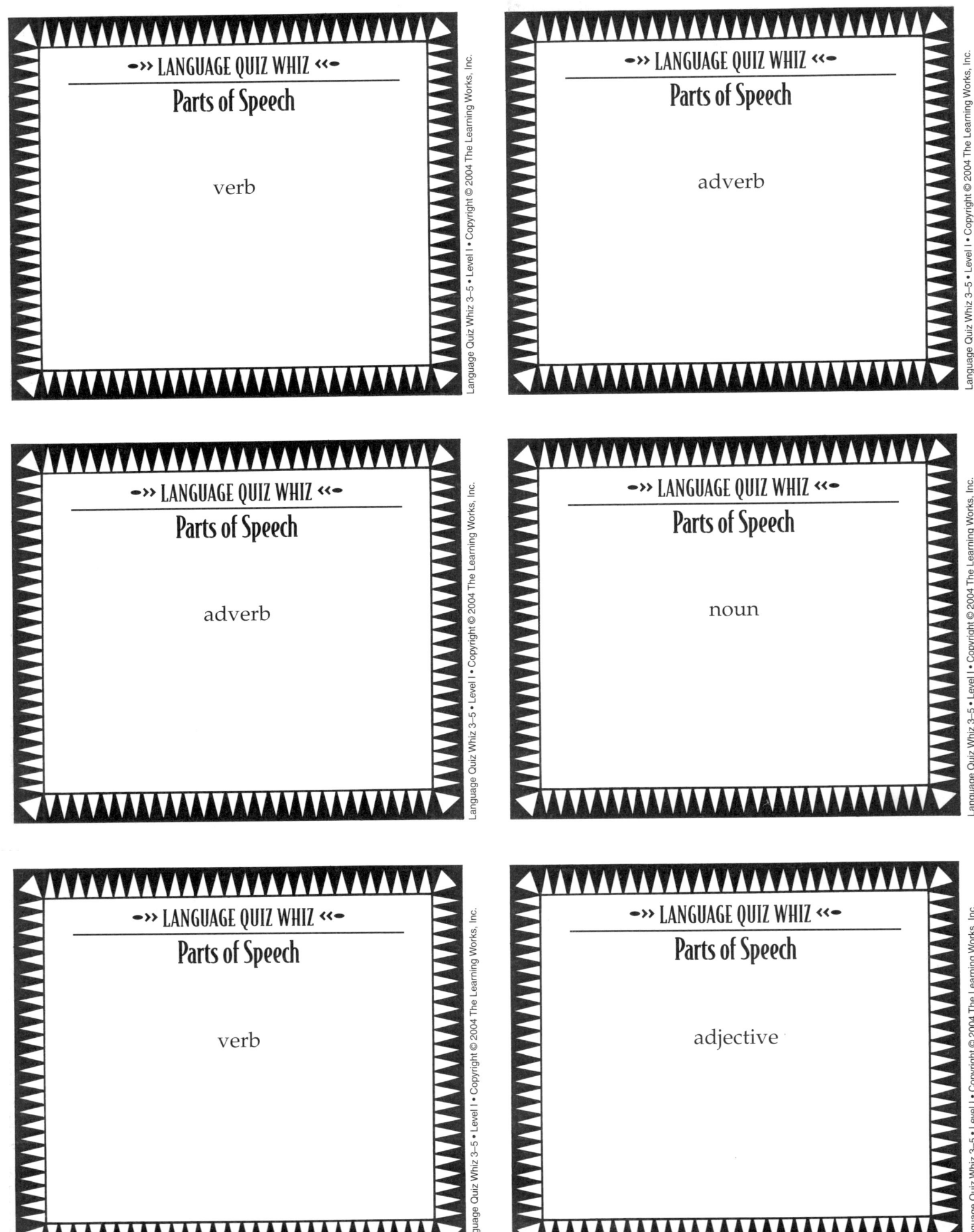

LANGUAGE QUIZ WHIZ
Parts of Speech

Which word is not a noun?

- myth
- mystery
- messy
- music

LANGUAGE QUIZ WHIZ
Parts of Speech

Which word is not an adjective?

- justly
- gloomy
- silky
- nervous

LANGUAGE QUIZ WHIZ
Parts of Speech

Which word is not an adverb?

- away
- nowhere
- everybody
- excitedly

LANGUAGE QUIZ WHIZ
Parts of Speech

Which word is not a verb?

- neither
- should
- are
- choose

LANGUAGE QUIZ WHIZ
Parts of Speech

Which word is not an interjection?

- oh
- ah
- if
- ugh

LANGUAGE QUIZ WHIZ
Parts of Speech

Which word is not a conjunction?

- and
- an
- but
- or

->> LANGUAGE QUIZ WHIZ <<-
Parts of Speech

What part of speech is the word *barely* in this sentence?

Dad was so tired after painting the room, he could *barely* move.

->> LANGUAGE QUIZ WHIZ <<-
Parts of Speech

What part of speech is the word *excuse* in this sentence?

Please *excuse* me for knocking over your glass.

->> LANGUAGE QUIZ WHIZ <<-
Parts of Speech

What part of speech is the word *whew* in this sentence?

Whew, that was a close call!

->> LANGUAGE QUIZ WHIZ <<-
Parts of Speech

What part of speech is the word *because* in this sentence?

She can't go with us *because* she is sick.

->> LANGUAGE QUIZ WHIZ <<-
Parts of Speech

What part of speech is the word *grill* in this sentence?

The hamburgers and hot dogs are on the *grill*.

->> LANGUAGE QUIZ WHIZ <<-
Parts of Speech

What part of speech is the word *ground* in this sentence?

My grandmother's apartment is on the *ground* floor.

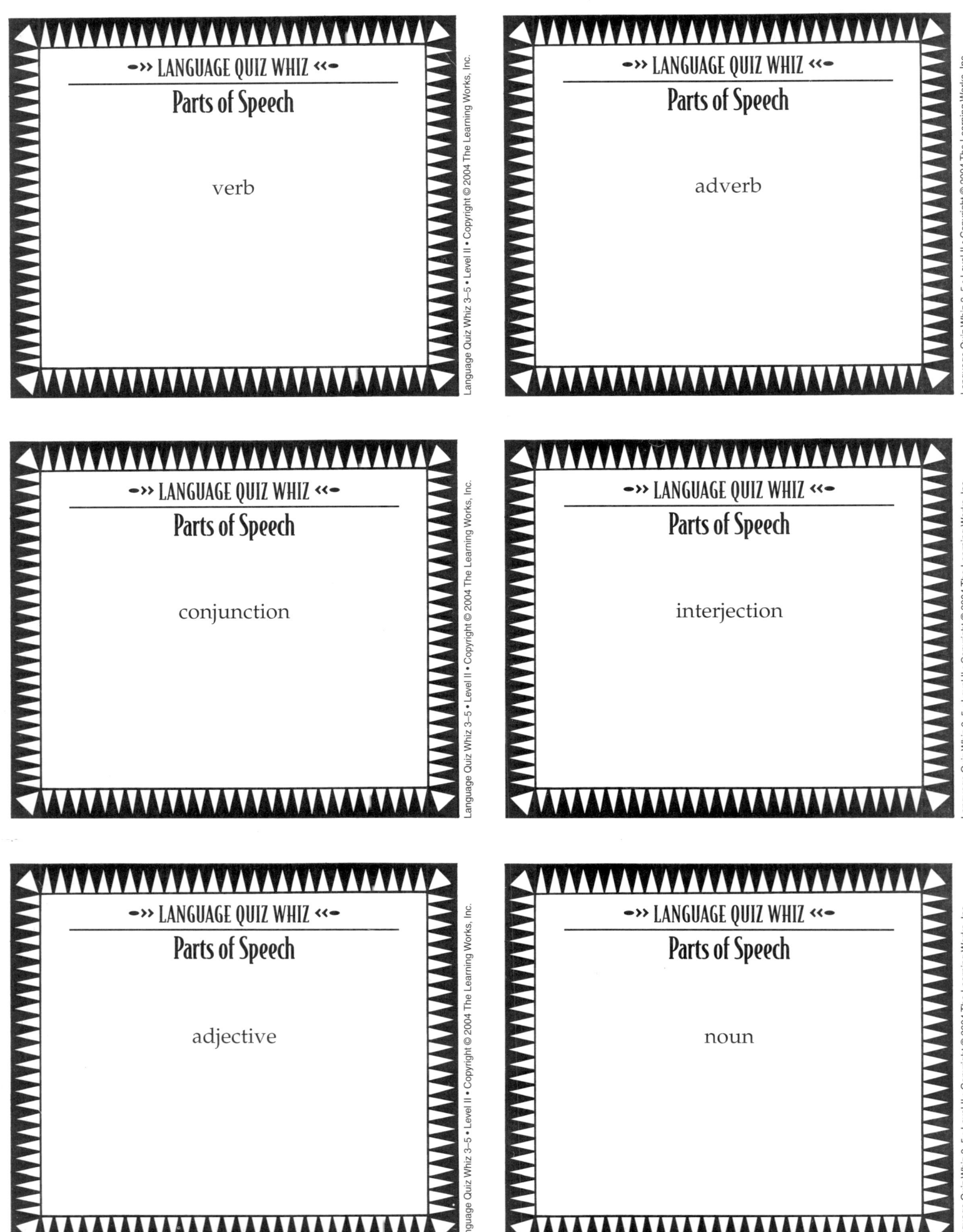

›› LANGUAGE QUIZ WHIZ ‹‹
Parts of Speech

Which word is not a verb?

    elevate
    elevator
    elect
    eliminate

›› LANGUAGE QUIZ WHIZ ‹‹
Parts of Speech

Which word is not an interjection?

    alas
    bah
    nor
    ouch

›› LANGUAGE QUIZ WHIZ ‹‹
Parts of Speech

Which word is not an adjective?

    misery
    hesitant
    lifeless
    muscular

›› LANGUAGE QUIZ WHIZ ‹‹
Parts of Speech

Which word is not a pronoun?

    somebody
    theirs
    between
    yourself

›› LANGUAGE QUIZ WHIZ ‹‹
Parts of Speech

Which word is not a preposition?

    through
    thought
    across
    upon

›› LANGUAGE QUIZ WHIZ ‹‹
Parts of Speech

Which word is not a verb?

    complaint
    compile
    compare
    coax

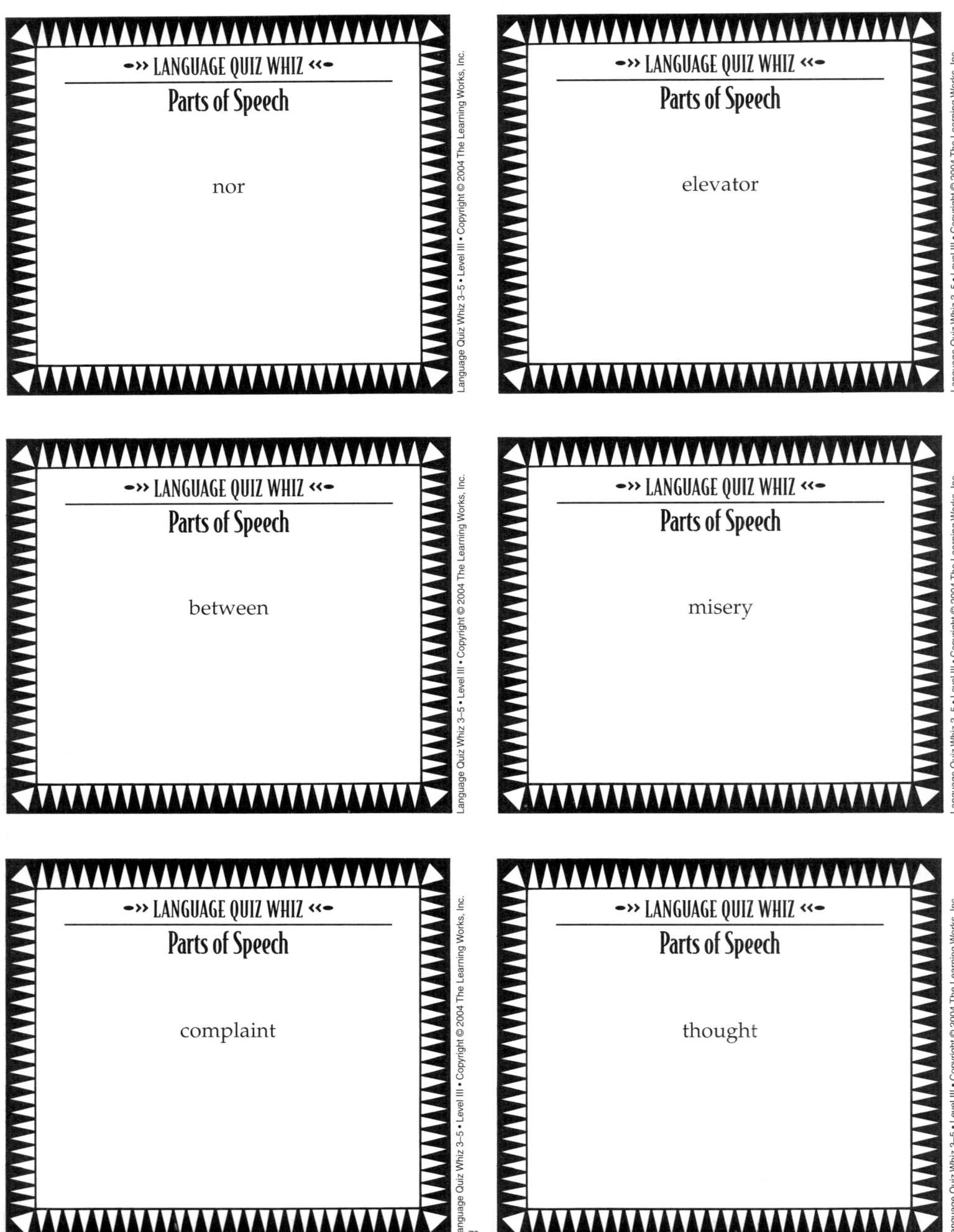

⇢» LANGUAGE QUIZ WHIZ «⇠
Parts of Speech

What part of speech is the word *harvest* in this sentence?

This is the season to *harvest* the crops.

⇢» LANGUAGE QUIZ WHIZ «⇠
Parts of Speech

What part of speech is the word *during* in this sentence?

It rained very hard *during* the night.

⇢» LANGUAGE QUIZ WHIZ «⇠
Parts of Speech

What part of speech is the word *capital* in this sentence?

What are your thoughts on the subject of *capital* punishment?

⇢» LANGUAGE QUIZ WHIZ «⇠
Parts of Speech

What part of speech is the word *tireless* in this sentence?

Mom won the award for her *tireless* effort in fund-raising.

⇢» LANGUAGE QUIZ WHIZ «⇠
Parts of Speech

What part of speech is the word *well* in this sentence?

Well, I have never heard such foolishness in my life!

⇢» LANGUAGE QUIZ WHIZ «⇠
Parts of Speech

What part of speech is the word *if* in this sentence?

I'd like to play soccer with you *if* I finish my homework.

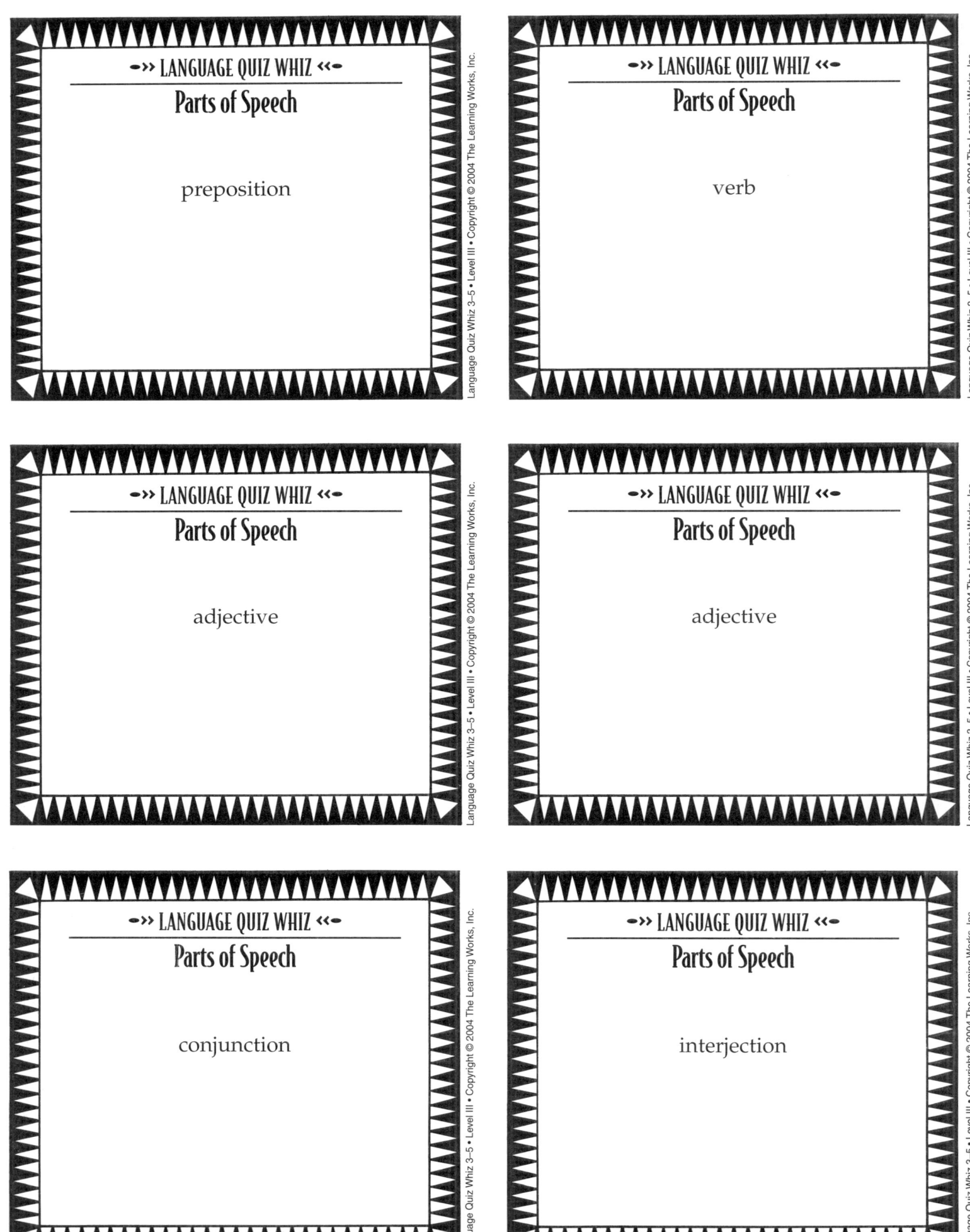

->» LANGUAGE QUIZ WHIZ «<-
Grammar

Which word does not use the article *an*?

  orange
  animal
  people
  elk

->» LANGUAGE QUIZ WHIZ «<-
Grammar

Fill in the missing word:

Dad ____ the mail on the kitchen counter.

  sat
  sit
  set

->» LANGUAGE QUIZ WHIZ «<-
Grammar

Fill in the missing word(s):

_____ many ways to solve the math problem.

  There is
  There are
  Their

->» LANGUAGE QUIZ WHIZ «<-
Grammar

Which of these words always uses a helping verb?

  know
  spoke
  taken

->» LANGUAGE QUIZ WHIZ «<-
Grammar

Fill in the missing word(s):

Yesterday I ____ chocolate milk for breakfast.

  drink
  drank
  have drunk

->» LANGUAGE QUIZ WHIZ «<-
Grammar

Which word does not use the article *a*?

  jury
  robot
  window
  octopus

→» LANGUAGE QUIZ WHIZ «←
Grammar

Which word is correct?

Yesterday I (run) (ran) home from school.

→» LANGUAGE QUIZ WHIZ «←
Grammar

Which word is correct?

(Begin) (Began) a sentence with a capital letter.

→» LANGUAGE QUIZ WHIZ «←
Grammar

Which word is correct?

I have (grew) (grown) two inches this year.

→» LANGUAGE QUIZ WHIZ «←
Grammar

Which word is correct?

I (knew) (known) the right answer.

→» LANGUAGE QUIZ WHIZ «←
Grammar

Which word is correct?

She (swim) (swam) in the lake.

→» LANGUAGE QUIZ WHIZ «←
Grammar

Which word is correct?

Dad has (wrote) (written) a check to pay for our new television.

LANGUAGE QUIZ WHIZ
Grammar

What is the past tense of the word *do*?

LANGUAGE QUIZ WHIZ
Grammar

What is the past tense of the word *know*?

LANGUAGE QUIZ WHIZ
Grammar

What is the past tense of the word *come*?

LANGUAGE QUIZ WHIZ
Grammar

What is the past tense of the word *rise*?

LANGUAGE QUIZ WHIZ
Grammar

What is the past tense of the word *wear*?

LANGUAGE QUIZ WHIZ
Grammar

What is the past tense of the word *ring*?

›› LANGUAGE QUIZ WHIZ ‹‹
Grammar

Which word is correct?

Of the two brothers, Jeff is the (more) (most) capable.

›› LANGUAGE QUIZ WHIZ ‹‹
Grammar

Which word is correct?

Of all the students in the class, Sarah is the (more) (most) talented.

›› LANGUAGE QUIZ WHIZ ‹‹
Grammar

Which word is correct?

There (is) (are) many books in our school library.

›› LANGUAGE QUIZ WHIZ ‹‹
Grammar

Which word is correct?

There (is) (are) only one lane of traffic open because of the accident.

›› LANGUAGE QUIZ WHIZ ‹‹
Grammar

Which word is correct?

Dad and I baked the pie (ourself) (ourselves).

›› LANGUAGE QUIZ WHIZ ‹‹
Grammar

Which word is correct?

She has (spoke) (spoken) to our scout troop before.

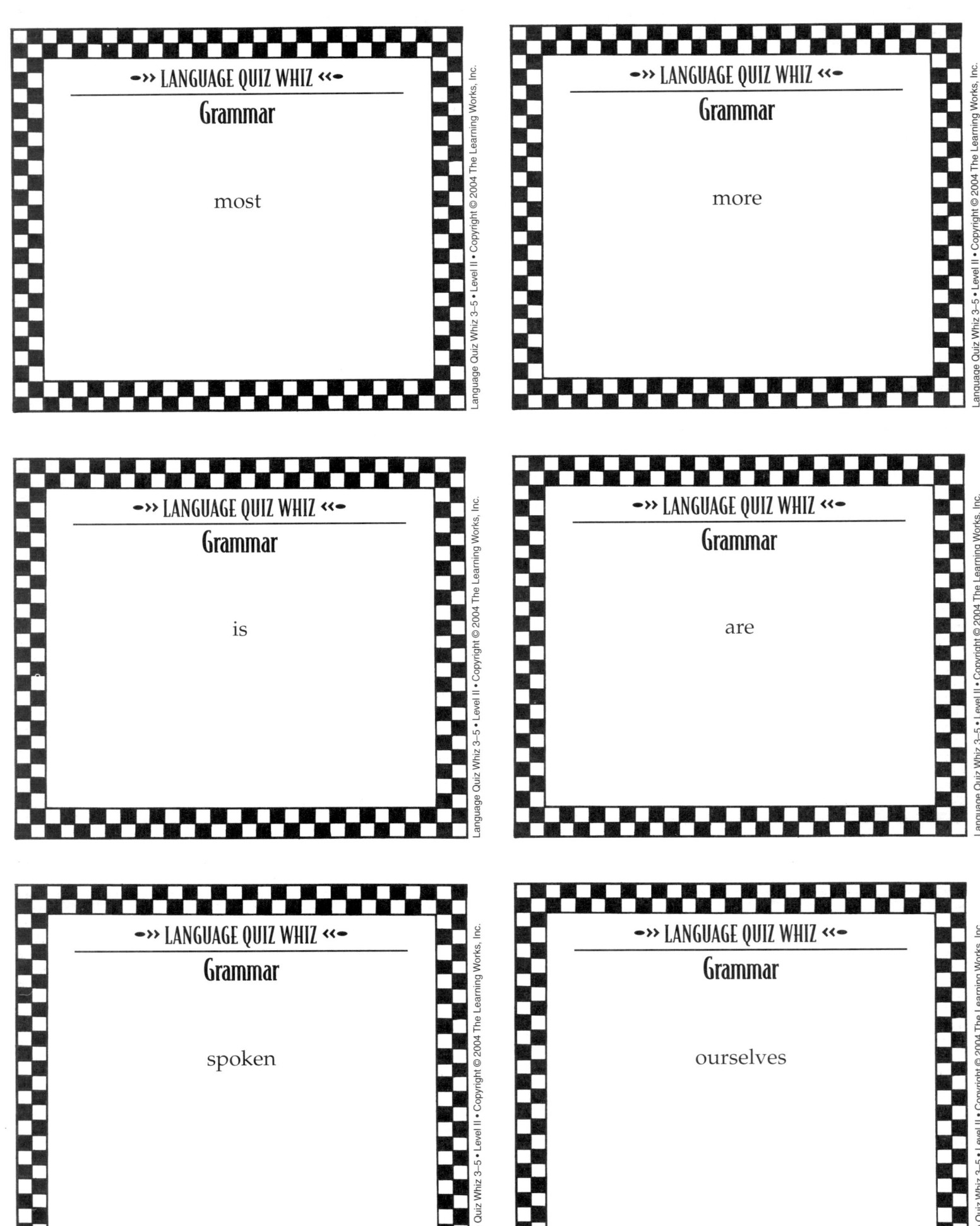

» LANGUAGE QUIZ WHIZ «
Grammar

Which word is correct?

(Neither) (Either) Steve nor Jose went to the party.

» LANGUAGE QUIZ WHIZ «
Grammar

Which word is correct?

The judges have (chose) (chosen) a winner.

» LANGUAGE QUIZ WHIZ «
Grammar

Which word is correct?

One of my favorite games (is) (are) chess.

» LANGUAGE QUIZ WHIZ «
Grammar

Which word is correct?

I have (forgot) (forgotten) her address.

» LANGUAGE QUIZ WHIZ «
Grammar

Which word is correct?

Gramps and (me) (I) went bowling yesterday.

» LANGUAGE QUIZ WHIZ «
Grammar

Which word is correct?

Pass the ball to (me) (I) if you get a chance.

LANGUAGE QUIZ WHIZ
Spelling

How do you spell the plural of *branch*?

LANGUAGE QUIZ WHIZ
Spelling

Which is the correct spelling?

delivor
deeliver
daliver
deliver

LANGUAGE QUIZ WHIZ
Spelling

How do you spell the contraction of the words *I am*?

LANGUAGE QUIZ WHIZ
Spelling

Which is the correct spelling?

ulways
always
allways
alwaze

LANGUAGE QUIZ WHIZ
Spelling

How do you spell the plural of *story*?

LANGUAGE QUIZ WHIZ
Spelling

How do you spell the plural of *roof*?

LANGUAGE QUIZ WHIZ
Spelling

deliver

LANGUAGE QUIZ WHIZ
Spelling

branches

LANGUAGE QUIZ WHIZ
Spelling

always

LANGUAGE QUIZ WHIZ
Spelling

I'm

LANGUAGE QUIZ WHIZ
Spelling

roofs

LANGUAGE QUIZ WHIZ
Spelling

stories

LANGUAGE QUIZ WHIZ
Spelling

How do you spell the contraction of the words *they are*?

LANGUAGE QUIZ WHIZ
Spelling

Which is the correct spelling?

wieght
waight
weight
wheit

LANGUAGE QUIZ WHIZ
Spelling

How do you spell the contraction of the words *she will*?

LANGUAGE QUIZ WHIZ
Spelling

Which is the correct spelling?

cheef
cheif
chief
chiefe

LANGUAGE QUIZ WHIZ
Spelling

How do you spell the contraction of the words *does not*?

LANGUAGE QUIZ WHIZ
Spelling

Which is the correct spelling?

success
sucess
succes
sukcess

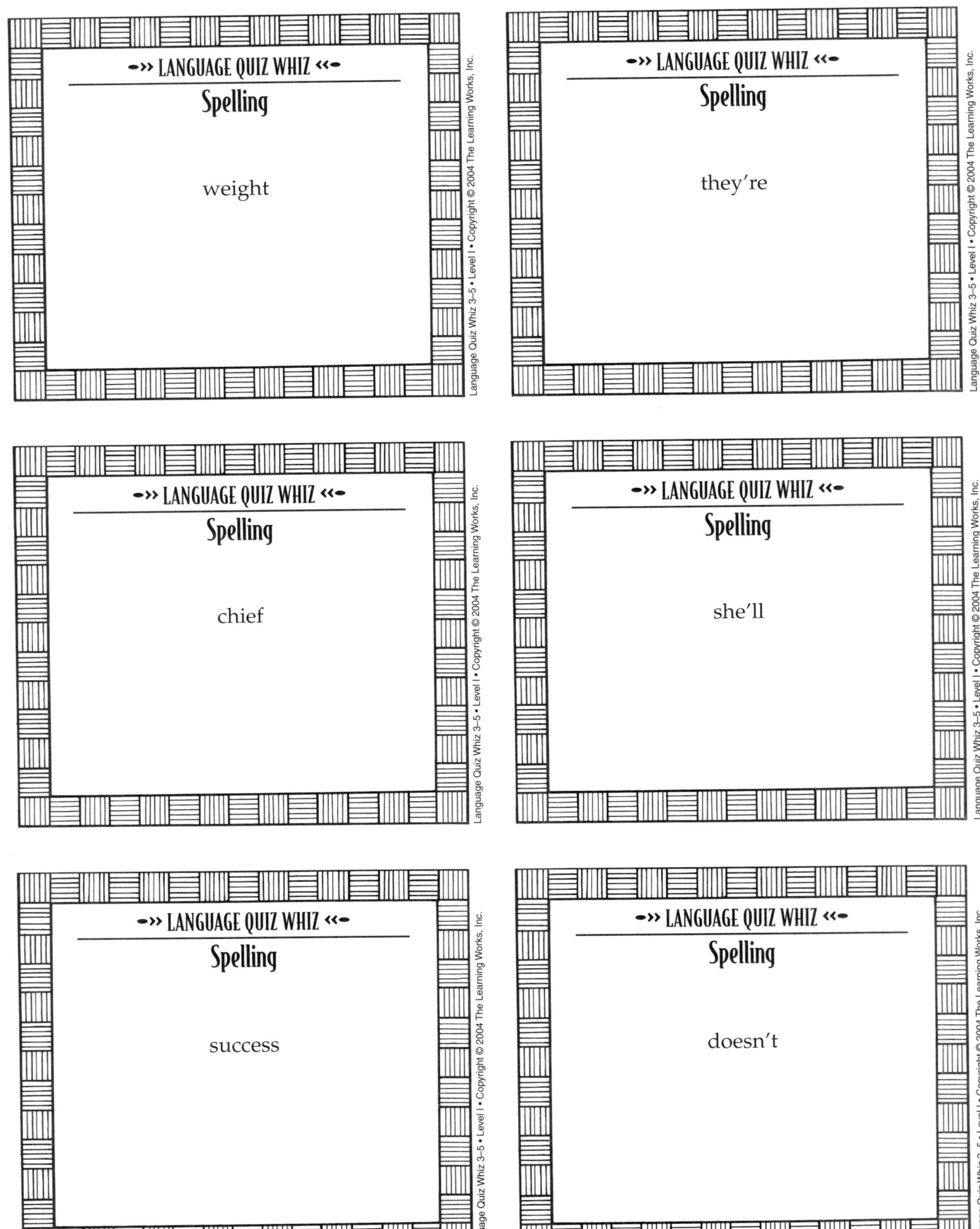

->> LANGUAGE QUIZ WHIZ <<-
Spelling

How do you spell the plural of *belief*?

->> LANGUAGE QUIZ WHIZ <<-
Spelling

Which is the correct spelling?

- buziness
- busines
- business
- buzines

->> LANGUAGE QUIZ WHIZ <<-
Spelling

How do you spell the plural of *veto*?

->> LANGUAGE QUIZ WHIZ <<-
Spelling

Which is the correct spelling?

- dictionery
- dictionary
- diktionery
- dicshunary

->> LANGUAGE QUIZ WHIZ <<-
Spelling

How do you spell the plural of *shelf*?

->> LANGUAGE QUIZ WHIZ <<-
Spelling

Which is the correct spelling?

- medicene
- midicine
- medicine
- medacine

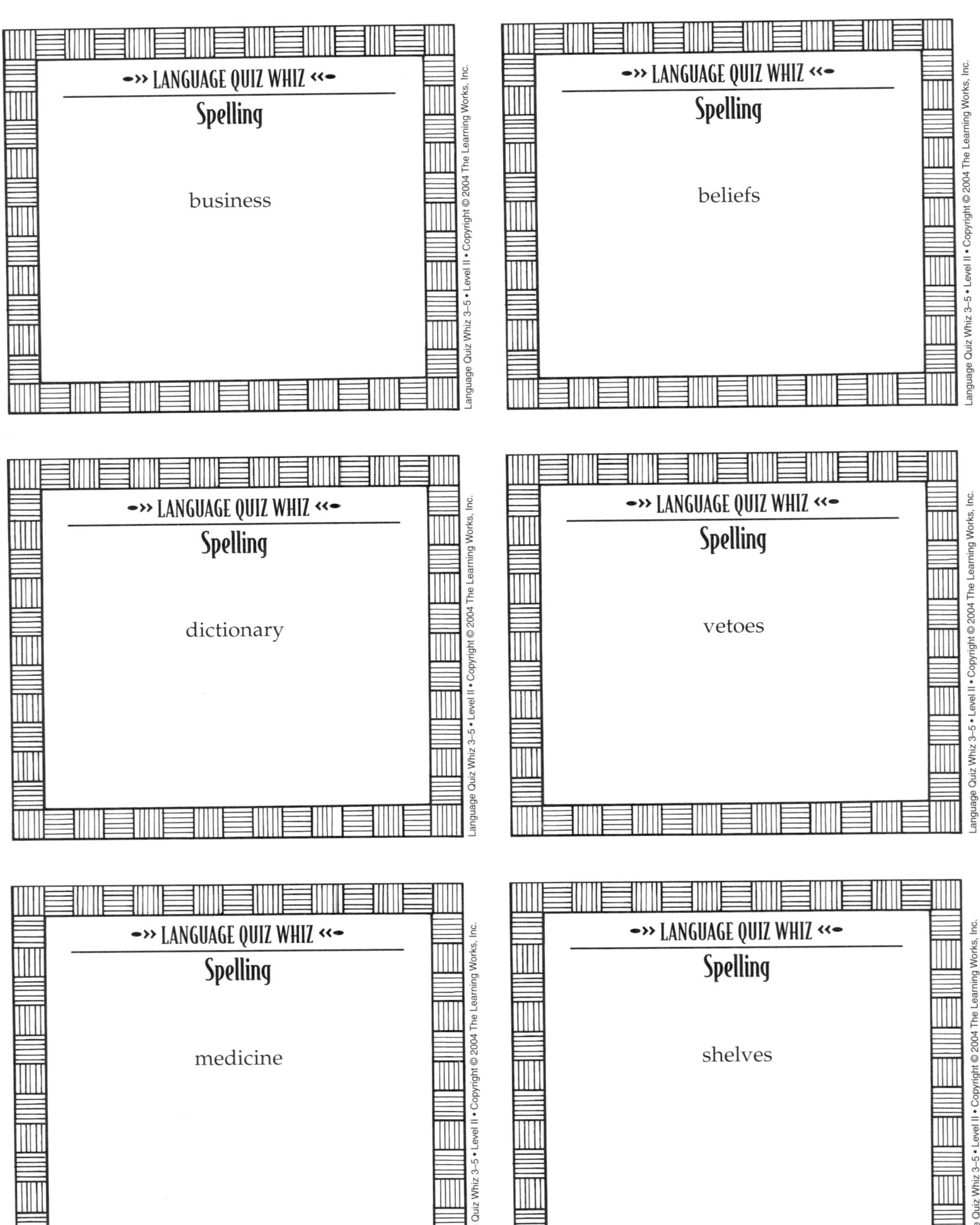

LANGUAGE QUIZ WHIZ
Spelling

How do you spell the plural of *cherry*?

LANGUAGE QUIZ WHIZ
Spelling

Which is the correct spelling?

differant
diferent
diffrant
different

LANGUAGE QUIZ WHIZ
Spelling

How do you spell the plural of *deer*?

LANGUAGE QUIZ WHIZ
Spelling

Which is the correct spelling?

seperate
separate
sepparate
sepurate

LANGUAGE QUIZ WHIZ
Spelling

How do you spell the plural of *tooth*?

LANGUAGE QUIZ WHIZ
Spelling

Which is the correct spelling?

comittee
comittee
committe
committee

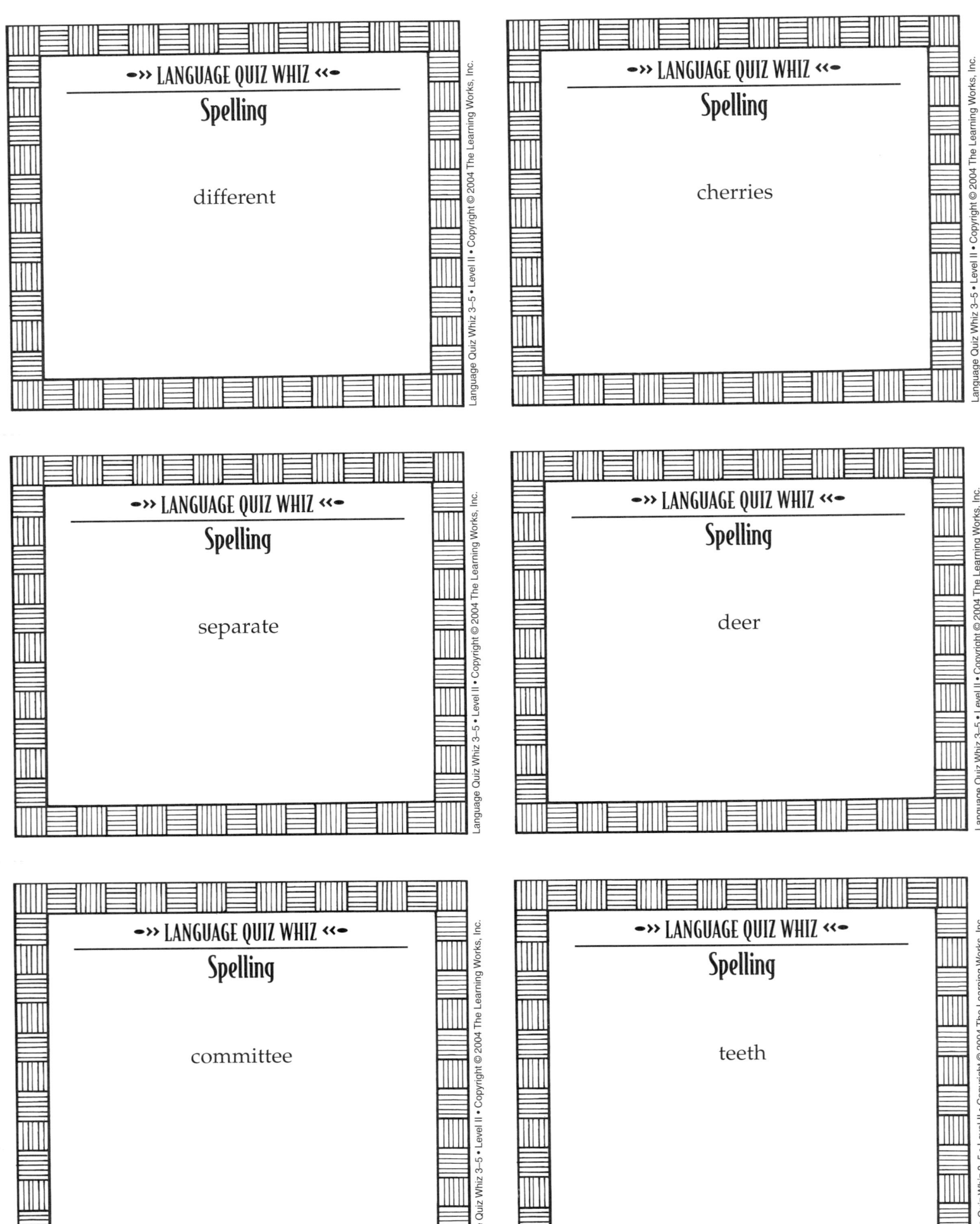

►» LANGUAGE QUIZ WHIZ «◄
Spelling

How do you spell the plural of *ox*?

►» LANGUAGE QUIZ WHIZ «◄
Spelling

Which is the correct spelling?

konvenience
conveneince
convenience
convenance

►» LANGUAGE QUIZ WHIZ «◄
Spelling

How do you spell the plural of *child*?

►» LANGUAGE QUIZ WHIZ «◄
Spelling

Which is the correct spelling?

occurrance
occurence
ocurrence
occurrence

►» LANGUAGE QUIZ WHIZ «◄
Spelling

How do you spell the plural of *cactus*?

►» LANGUAGE QUIZ WHIZ «◄
Spelling

Which is the correct spelling?

accommodate
acommodate
accomodate
acomodate

LANGUAGE QUIZ WHIZ
Spelling

convenience

LANGUAGE QUIZ WHIZ
Spelling

oxen

LANGUAGE QUIZ WHIZ
Spelling

occurrence

LANGUAGE QUIZ WHIZ
Spelling

children

LANGUAGE QUIZ WHIZ
Spelling

accommodate

LANGUAGE QUIZ WHIZ
Spelling

cacti; cactuses

LANGUAGE QUIZ WHIZ
Spelling

How do you spell the plural of *salmon*?

LANGUAGE QUIZ WHIZ
Spelling

Which is the correct spelling?

owkward
awkwerd
awkward
awkword

LANGUAGE QUIZ WHIZ
Spelling

How do you spell the plural of *portfolio*?

LANGUAGE QUIZ WHIZ
Spelling

Which is the correct spelling?

embarasment
embarrassment
embarassment
embarrasment

LANGUAGE QUIZ WHIZ
Spelling

How do you spell the plural of *octopus*?

LANGUAGE QUIZ WHIZ
Spelling

Which is the correct spelling?

correspondence
correspondance
corespondance
corespondence

Language Quiz Whiz — Spelling

awkward

Language Quiz Whiz — Spelling

salmon

Language Quiz Whiz — Spelling

embarrassment

Language Quiz Whiz — Spelling

portfolios

Language Quiz Whiz — Spelling

correspondence

Language Quiz Whiz — Spelling

octopi; octopuses

·›› LANGUAGE QUIZ WHIZ ‹‹·
Literature

What is the page of a book called that gives the title and name of the author, illustrator, and publisher?

·›› LANGUAGE QUIZ WHIZ ‹‹·
Literature

What are the first names of the brother and sister who get lost in the woods and discover a house made of candy?

·›› LANGUAGE QUIZ WHIZ ‹‹·
Literature

What word is missing from the title of this book written by Eric Carle: *The Very Hungry _____* ?

·›› LANGUAGE QUIZ WHIZ ‹‹·
Literature

What is the first name of the young boy who planted seeds, climbed a beanstalk, and met a giant?

·›› LANGUAGE QUIZ WHIZ ‹‹·
Literature

What word is missing from the title of this book written by Margery Williams: *The Velveteen ____* ?

·›› LANGUAGE QUIZ WHIZ ‹‹·
Literature

What is the name of the bear in A.A. Milne's popular books?

LANGUAGE QUIZ WHIZ
Literature

Hansel and Gretel

LANGUAGE QUIZ WHIZ
Literature

the title page

LANGUAGE QUIZ WHIZ
Literature

Jack

LANGUAGE QUIZ WHIZ
Literature

Caterpillar

LANGUAGE QUIZ WHIZ
Literature

Winnie-the-Pooh

LANGUAGE QUIZ WHIZ
Literature

Rabbit

LANGUAGE QUIZ WHIZ
Literature

What is the name of the rat in the book *Charlotte's Web* by E.B. White?

LANGUAGE QUIZ WHIZ
Literature

What word is missing from the title of this book written by Maurice Sendak: *In the ____ Kitchen*?

LANGUAGE QUIZ WHIZ
Literature

What is a written work that tells a story about characters and events that are not real called?

LANGUAGE QUIZ WHIZ
Literature

Who is the author of *The Tale of Peter Rabbit*?

LANGUAGE QUIZ WHIZ
Literature

What word is missing from the title of this book: *____ and the Beast*?

LANGUAGE QUIZ WHIZ
Literature

Who is the author of *The Cat in the Hat*?

LANGUAGE QUIZ WHIZ
Literature

Night

LANGUAGE QUIZ WHIZ
Literature

Templeton

LANGUAGE QUIZ WHIZ
Literature

Beatrix Potter

LANGUAGE QUIZ WHIZ
Literature

fiction

LANGUAGE QUIZ WHIZ
Literature

Dr. Seuss
(Theodor Geisel)

LANGUAGE QUIZ WHIZ
Literature

Beauty

LANGUAGE QUIZ WHIZ
Literature

What page in the front of a book lists the important parts by title and page number in the order in which they appear?

LANGUAGE QUIZ WHIZ
Literature

What is the name of the girl who falls down a rabbit hole in a book by Lewis Carroll?

LANGUAGE QUIZ WHIZ
Literature

What color word is missing from the title of this Newbery Medal-winning book by Scott O'Dell: *Island of the _____ Dolphins*?

LANGUAGE QUIZ WHIZ
Literature

What is writing that is not fiction and deals with real people and events called?

LANGUAGE QUIZ WHIZ
Literature

Who wrote the books *Ramona the Pest* and *Dear Mr. Henshaw*?

LANGUAGE QUIZ WHIZ
Literature

Is the main part of a book called the glossary, the index, the body, or the copyright?

LANGUAGE QUIZ WHIZ
Literature

Alice
(*Alice in Wonderland*)

LANGUAGE QUIZ WHIZ
Literature

the table of contents

LANGUAGE QUIZ WHIZ
Literature

nonfiction

LANGUAGE QUIZ WHIZ
Literature

Blue

LANGUAGE QUIZ WHIZ
Literature

the body

LANGUAGE QUIZ WHIZ
Literature

Beverly Cleary

LANGUAGE QUIZ WHIZ
Literature

In the book *Shiloh* by Phyllis Naylor, what kind of animal is Shiloh?

LANGUAGE QUIZ WHIZ
Literature

Who is the author of the Harry Potter series?

LANGUAGE QUIZ WHIZ
Literature

Who wrote the book *Where the Sidewalk Ends,* a collection of humorous poems?

LANGUAGE QUIZ WHIZ
Literature

What word is missing from the title of this Hans Christian Andersen book: *The ___ New Clothes*?

LANGUAGE QUIZ WHIZ
Literature

Who is the author of *Tiger Eyes* and *Tales of a Fourth Grade Nothing*?

LANGUAGE QUIZ WHIZ
Literature

What part of a book, usually found in the back, is an alphabetical list of the topics covered along with the numbers of the pages on which they are defined?

LANGUAGE QUIZ WHIZ
Literature

J.K. Rowling

LANGUAGE QUIZ WHIZ
Literature

a dog

LANGUAGE QUIZ WHIZ
Literature

Emperor's

LANGUAGE QUIZ WHIZ
Literature

Shel Silverstein

LANGUAGE QUIZ WHIZ
Literature

the index

LANGUAGE QUIZ WHIZ
Literature

Judy Blume

» LANGUAGE QUIZ WHIZ «
Literature

Who owned the factory in Roald Dahl's book *Charlie and the Chocolate Factory*?

» LANGUAGE QUIZ WHIZ «
Literature

What is an alphabetical listing of difficult, special, or technical words used in a book with their definitions and often their pronunciations called?

» LANGUAGE QUIZ WHIZ «
Literature

What is the title of Louisa May Alcott's book about four sisters?

» LANGUAGE QUIZ WHIZ «
Literature

Who wrote *The Adventures of Tom Sawyer*?

» LANGUAGE QUIZ WHIZ «
Literature

What part of a book, often the back of the title page, includes the copyright notice, the name of the publishing company or person holding the copyright, and the year in which the book was copyrighted?

» LANGUAGE QUIZ WHIZ «
Literature

Who is the author of the Newbery Medal-winning book *Crispin: The Cross of Lead*?

LANGUAGE QUIZ WHIZ
Literature

a glossary

LANGUAGE QUIZ WHIZ
Literature

Willy Wonka

LANGUAGE QUIZ WHIZ
Literature

Mark Twain
(Samuel Clemens)

LANGUAGE QUIZ WHIZ
Literature

Little Women

LANGUAGE QUIZ WHIZ
Literature

Avi

LANGUAGE QUIZ WHIZ
Literature

the copyright page

LANGUAGE QUIZ WHIZ
Literature

What is the name of the Newbery Medal-winning author of *Number the Stars*?

LANGUAGE QUIZ WHIZ
Literature

What word is missing from the title of this Newbery Medal-winning book by Sharon Creech: *Walk Two ___*?

LANGUAGE QUIZ WHIZ
Literature

What do you call a book about a person's life written by that person?

LANGUAGE QUIZ WHIZ
Literature

What word is missing from the title of this Newbery Medal-winning book by Katherine Paterson: *___ to Terabithia*?

LANGUAGE QUIZ WHIZ
Literature

What do you call a book about a person's life written by another person?

LANGUAGE QUIZ WHIZ
Literature

What boy's name is missing from the title of this Newbery Medal-winning book by Jerry Spinelli: *Maniac ___*?

LANGUAGE QUIZ WHIZ
Literature

Moons

LANGUAGE QUIZ WHIZ
Literature

Lois Lowry

LANGUAGE QUIZ WHIZ
Literature

Bridge

LANGUAGE QUIZ WHIZ
Literature

an autobiography

LANGUAGE QUIZ WHIZ
Literature

Magee

LANGUAGE QUIZ WHIZ
Literature

a biography

›› LANGUAGE QUIZ WHIZ ‹‹
Odd Word Out

Which word does not belong?

    bowling
    field
    wrestling
    soccer

›› LANGUAGE QUIZ WHIZ ‹‹
Odd Word Out

Which word does not belong?

    it's
    mine
    they'll
    he's

›› LANGUAGE QUIZ WHIZ ‹‹
Odd Word Out

Which word does not belong?

    oboe
    trumpet
    tenor
    piano

›› LANGUAGE QUIZ WHIZ ‹‹
Odd Word Out

Which word does not belong?

    north
    east
    map
    west

›› LANGUAGE QUIZ WHIZ ‹‹
Odd Word Out

Which word does not belong?

    wharf
    runway
    luggage
    jet

›› LANGUAGE QUIZ WHIZ ‹‹
Odd Word Out

Which word does not belong?

    Mrs.
    Mar.
    Dec.
    Feb.

LANGUAGE QUIZ WHIZ
Odd Word Out

mine
(not a contraction)

LANGUAGE QUIZ WHIZ
Odd Word Out

field
(not a sport)

LANGUAGE QUIZ WHIZ
Odd Word Out

map
(not the name of a direction)

LANGUAGE QUIZ WHIZ
Odd Word Out

tenor
(not a musical instrument)

LANGUAGE QUIZ WHIZ
Odd Word Out

Mrs.
(not an abbreviation
for a month of the year)

LANGUAGE QUIZ WHIZ
Odd Word Out

wharf
(not something
found in an airport)

»> LANGUAGE QUIZ WHIZ «<
Odd Word Out

Which word does not belong?

- judge
- teacher
- principal
- secretary

»> LANGUAGE QUIZ WHIZ «<
Odd Word Out

Which word does not belong?

- moon
- noon
- planet
- star

»> LANGUAGE QUIZ WHIZ «<
Odd Word Out

Which word does not belong?

- huge
- tiny
- enormous
- gigantic

»> LANGUAGE QUIZ WHIZ «<
Odd Word Out

Which word does not belong?

- third
- quarter
- nickel
- dime

»> LANGUAGE QUIZ WHIZ «<
Odd Word Out

Which word does not belong?

- shoe
- giraffe
- telephone
- beautiful

»> LANGUAGE QUIZ WHIZ «<
Odd Word Out

Which word does not belong?

- heart
- diamond
- skin
- lung

LANGUAGE QUIZ WHIZ
Odd Word Out

noon
(not found in the sky)

LANGUAGE QUIZ WHIZ
Odd Word Out

judge
(not a person who works in a school)

LANGUAGE QUIZ WHIZ
Odd Word Out

third
(not the name of a coin)

LANGUAGE QUIZ WHIZ
Odd Word Out

tiny
(not a synonym for the other words that mean *very large*)

LANGUAGE QUIZ WHIZ
Odd Word Out

diamond
(not an organ found in the body)

LANGUAGE QUIZ WHIZ
Odd Word Out

beautiful
(not a noun)

›› LANGUAGE QUIZ WHIZ ‹‹
Odd Word Out

Which word does not belong?

- comma
- common
- period
- colon

›› LANGUAGE QUIZ WHIZ ‹‹
Odd Word Out

Which word does not belong?

- women
- mice
- teeth
- child

›› LANGUAGE QUIZ WHIZ ‹‹
Odd Word Out

Which word does not belong?

- avenue
- sidewalk
- lane
- street

›› LANGUAGE QUIZ WHIZ ‹‹
Odd Word Out

Which word does not belong?

- archery
- soccer
- basketball
- tennis

›› LANGUAGE QUIZ WHIZ ‹‹
Odd Word Out

Which word does not belong?

- adj.
- adv.
- pron.
- Oct.

›› LANGUAGE QUIZ WHIZ ‹‹
Odd Word Out

Which word does not belong?

- broil
- fry
- bake
- dive

LANGUAGE QUIZ WHIZ
Odd Word Out

child
(not a plural form of a word)

LANGUAGE QUIZ WHIZ
Odd Word Out

common
(not a punctuation mark)

LANGUAGE QUIZ WHIZ
Odd Word Out

archery
(not played with a ball)

LANGUAGE QUIZ WHIZ
Odd Word Out

sidewalk
(not part of an address)

LANGUAGE QUIZ WHIZ
Odd Word Out

dive
(not a way to prepare or cook food)

LANGUAGE QUIZ WHIZ
Odd Word Out

Oct.
(not an abbreviation for a part of speech)

LANGUAGE QUIZ WHIZ
Odd Word Out

Which word does not belong?

    banjo
    guitar
    music
    ukulele

LANGUAGE QUIZ WHIZ
Odd Word Out

Which word does not belong?

    elves
    potatoes
    bushes
    cargo

LANGUAGE QUIZ WHIZ
Odd Word Out

Which word does not belong?

    vain
    very
    vane
    vein

LANGUAGE QUIZ WHIZ
Odd Word Out

Which word does not belong?

    mission
    modem
    mouse
    menu

LANGUAGE QUIZ WHIZ
Odd Word Out

Which word does not belong?

    oven
    shower
    sink
    stove

LANGUAGE QUIZ WHIZ
Odd Word Out

Which word does not belong?

    ambulance
    canoe
    bus
    garage

LANGUAGE QUIZ WHIZ
Odd Word Out

cargo
(not a plural)

LANGUAGE QUIZ WHIZ
Odd Word Out

music
(not an instrument)

LANGUAGE QUIZ WHIZ
Odd Word Out

mission
(not a computer term)

LANGUAGE QUIZ WHIZ
Odd Word Out

very
(not a homophone)

LANGUAGE QUIZ WHIZ
Odd Word Out

garage
(not a form of transportation)

LANGUAGE QUIZ WHIZ
Odd Word Out

shower
(not something found in a kitchen)

» LANGUAGE QUIZ WHIZ «
Odd Word Out

Which word does not belong?

  them
  children
  her
  ourselves

» LANGUAGE QUIZ WHIZ «
Odd Word Out

Which word does not belong?

  place
  across
  to
  outside

» LANGUAGE QUIZ WHIZ «
Odd Word Out

Which word does not belong?

  fireplace
  outline
  sentence
  sunshine

» LANGUAGE QUIZ WHIZ «
Odd Word Out

Which word does not belong?

  mellow
  resourceful
  obvious
  eliminate

» LANGUAGE QUIZ WHIZ «
Odd Word Out

Which word does not belong?

  drawn
  grow
  shaken
  frozen

» LANGUAGE QUIZ WHIZ «
Odd Word Out

Which word does not belong?

  limbo
  samba
  flamenco
  ballad

LANGUAGE QUIZ WHIZ
Odd Word Out

place
(not a preposition)

LANGUAGE QUIZ WHIZ
Odd Word Out

children
(not a pronoun)

LANGUAGE QUIZ WHIZ
Odd Word Out

eliminate
(not an adjective)

LANGUAGE QUIZ WHIZ
Odd Word Out

sentence
(not a compound word)

LANGUAGE QUIZ WHIZ
Odd Word Out

ballad
(not a type of dance)

LANGUAGE QUIZ WHIZ
Odd Word Out

grow
(not a past participle)

—» LANGUAGE QUIZ WHIZ «—
Odd Word Out

dribble
(not a football term)

—» LANGUAGE QUIZ WHIZ «—
Odd Word Out

braid
(not the name of something that holds things)

—» LANGUAGE QUIZ WHIZ «—
Odd Word Out

investigate
(not a compound word)

—» LANGUAGE QUIZ WHIZ «—
Odd Word Out

lily
(not an adverb)

—» LANGUAGE QUIZ WHIZ «—
Odd Word Out

library
(not part of a book)

—» LANGUAGE QUIZ WHIZ «—
Odd Word Out

lace
(not the name of a color)

→» LANGUAGE QUIZ WHIZ «←
Odd Word Out

Which word does not belong?

crimson
lace
magenta
khaki

→» LANGUAGE QUIZ WHIZ «←
Odd Word Out

Which word does not belong?

library
preface
glossary
bibliography

→» LANGUAGE QUIZ WHIZ «←
Odd Word Out

Which word does not belong?

moderately
sharply
excitedly
lily

→» LANGUAGE QUIZ WHIZ «←
Odd Word Out

Which word does not belong?

bookworm
input
investigate
skateboard

→» LANGUAGE QUIZ WHIZ «←
Odd Word Out

Which word does not belong?

braid
bucket
basket
bag

→» LANGUAGE QUIZ WHIZ «←
Odd Word Out

Which word does not belong?

kickoff
punt
tackle
dribble